DEADLIER
THAN
THE MALE

wensley clarkson

BLAKE

Published by Blake Publishing Ltd,
3 Bramber Court, 2 Bramber Road,
London W14 9PB, England

First published in 1999

ISBN 1 85782 377 X

British Library Cataloguing-in-Publication Data:
A catalogue record for this book is available
from the British Library.

Typeset by BCP

Printed in Great Britain by
Creative Print and Design (Wales), Ebbw Vale, Gwent

3 5 7 9 10 8 6 4 2

To every woman
who has ever lost her temper
with her man.

Contents

Dear Reader

Welcome to the first title in Blake's True Crime Library. Every month we will be bringing you the latest, most sensational true crime that will take you straight to the heart of the most horrific crimes and into the minds of the world's most notorious criminals.

Wensley Clarkson is the country's foremost investigative crime-writer, whose research into the shadowy world of female killers has led him to probe deeply into the disturbed psyche of some of the world's most depraved women. In this revelatory book he reveals the grisly truth behind their crimes and examines the motives that drive such women to commit such gruesome acts of violence. The conclusions he draws are genuinely startling — even more so because every word is true!

This is a book that will chill your blood, and which will force you to ask yourself if the female of the species really is ... Deadlier than the Male!

Adam Parfitt
Editor
Blake's True Crime Library

1

Crime of Passion

Paul Birch loved his job. Each morning he would walk briskly across the road from his neat suburban home in Kingston, Surrey, to his office just a few hundred yards away. It was so much more pleasant than facing one of those long traffic-congested journey or sardine-packed train rides into London.

The work itself was an art form, according to Paul. A carefully nurtured skill that took years and years of training. Now, at 33 years of age, he was at the peak of his profession. Each of his customers was a fresh challenge that had to be faced with equal enthusiasm.

Paul was also very proud of his job. He saw it as a vital service to the community and, in many ways, it was hard to disagree with him. But then embalming is one of those professions that many people would rather not hear about or see too much of. Even in these modern times, attitudes towards death are still tinged with fear despite the fact that it happens to us all in the end.

As one prominent member of the undertaking trade once said: 'This is the only business in the world where everyone is a potential customer.'

Paul himself had a definite way with people — both dead and alive. An unassuming, prematurely balding man with soft brown eyes and a very gentle manner, he had a reputation amongst local funeral parlours as being one hell of a good professional. He really did seem concerned that those grieving loved ones were treated with warmth rather than distance by their undertakers.

A lot of his colleagues put all this down to the fact that he had not taken the traditional route to the funeral business, which is filled with families that go back three, four, even five generations. No, Paul Birch had even enjoyed a spell in the army before buying himself out in 1979. He had, as they say, lived a full life, and many believed that made him all the more sensitive towards his clients.

Paul explained his unusual choice of a second career by saying he had always been fascinated by the 'business' and he saw it as a genuine service to the community. He was delighted when he qualified as an embalmer and joined the prestigious British Institute of Embalmers at the tender age of 26. It had taken him just a year of careful training to reach that first step in his ambitious career in the world of death.

Throughout all this there was his gregarious, bubbly hairdresser wife Julie. They had first met when he was stationed in West Germany in the forces. Paul was just 24 years old and she was twelve years his senior. But none of that mattered. They had been instantly attracted. Julie's stunning West Indian looks were quite an eye-opener in the grim Bavarian countryside where Paul was based at the time. Soon she was teaching Paul things about lovemaking that he never knew existed.

Julie — or "Beulah" as her family had christened her — was a very experienced woman in every sense. She had been married before and was the mother of three children, but she still retained a sense of fun that Paul had never come across before. She had a live-for-today attitude that he found truly magnetic. Happiness was her main priority. She desperately wanted to make Paul equally content.

When Paul quit the services, they soon settled in a modest, but very comfortable flat in Horace Road, Kingston. He pursued his career in the funeral business and Julie made great inroads into the hairdressing profession and was soon managing the B. Casual salon on the nearby Cambridge Housing Estate.

Horace Road was a pretty stodgy street when it wanted to be. Your run-of-the-mill lower-middle-class assortment of houses and flats built mainly between the wars. A breeding ground for die-hard bigots.

The sight of the handsome young man and his much older, West Indian wife was hardly greeted with enthusiasm by the locals. Many neighbours fully expected calypso parties and cannabis plants in the garden. The truth was that Julie and Paul were a rather charming couple who got on with their lives in a very hardworking, studious sort of way. Both of them were up early every day, worked long hours and came back to the flat to enjoy romantic candle-lit dinners before retiring to bed for an early night.

To start with, hardly any of the neighbours even said good morning as Paul and Julie ventured out on their way to work. But gradually they became accepted by the other residents, much to their surprise.

But being involved in a mixed-race marriage taught Paul a lot more about life. It opened his eyes to the short-sighted prejudices that exist and it sparked his interest in local politics. You see, Paul Birch wanted to do his bit to change the world. He began to nurture great political aspirations, and they soon manifested themselves in his application to join the local Labour Party.

But he did not stop there. Next he put himself up for election to the local council and, in an area that included a couple of vast council housing estates with high rises, he easily got in. Within a few years of arriving in Kingston, the Birches had become a very well known local couple. Soon their black and white 'coalition' seemed irrelevant. By 1986, they were seen as a very glamorous pair. Now it was more than just their neighbours who were greeting them in the street.

Throughout all this, Paul also managed to build his reputation as one of the finest embalmers in Surrey. His job at the Lear of London firm was pretty unique because he was given the official title of 'Mobile Embalmer'. In short, wherever there was a corpse that needed attending to, Paul Birch, complete with radio pager, would be sent.

He prided himself on his ability to 'rebuild' the most horrifically injured bodies to their former glory, so that loved ones could take one last look at their deceased relatives and know they were going to a better world looking fit and healthy enough to be accepted.

Paul appreciated just how important it was to make those corpses look almost as good as new — even though they were more often than not only laid out for a few hours before being lowered to the ground or turned to ashes for eternity.

His bosses at Lear were delighted that Paul's political career was going so well. They saw his success as a great way to spread the word about the funeral business. Bring it more out in the open for everyone to see and hear about.

And when Paul announced he was standing as the Labour Party candidate for Kingston in 1986, they were over the moon. The undertaking business had always been hidden behind blacked-out shop windows and talked about in hushed whispers. Now here was a man standing on a platform telling the world that he was an embalmer — and proud of it!

Sadly, Paul Birch's bid for real political power failed when he lost out to the Tory opposition. But at least he had made his mark on local party politics. He had become a real force to be reckoned with.

Meanwhile, attractive Julie was busy behind the scenes working at her hairdressing salon and returning home each night to make her man feel happy in every way possible. And Julie knew that the best way to a man's heart was through his stomach. She loved cooking huge stews and rice dishes that he had grown to really enjoy.

But over the road from their neat little flat, Paul Birch was juggling more than just his career as an embalmer with those deep-set political aspirations. His recently discovered local fame had put him on a pedestal at Lear's of London — and for the first time in his life he was attracting the sort of attention only unmarried men are supposed to revel in.

Their rubber-gloved hands just brushed each other ever so slightly. Through that white see-through material it might have meant nothing. After all, they were just about to carry out a full embalmment on a body that lay on a slab in front of them. Then he caught her glance and realised exactly what was going through her mind.

But still he said nothing and — like the true professional he was — he started the gruesome task that lay before them. As they moved the corpse over on its stomach her eyes caught him head on again. Paul Birch coughed. It was a sign of embarrassment really. He wanted to somehow let her know that he knew. But he did not really know how to handle the situation. However, he was fully aware of one thing — if Julie ever found out, she would become insanely jealous. He had never forgotten how she warned him once that if he was ever unfaithful she would 'shoot your balls to bits'.

Most women might not have meant it. But Julie was not like any other female he had ever met. Somehow, he suspected that she meant every word.

Despite his wife's warning ringing in his ears, Paul Birch was finding it very difficult to resist his colleague. It is probably hard to imagine how anyone could find such grisly surroundings in the least bit romantic, but when you've worked under such circumstances for many years you become immune to the smell and feel of a corpse.

As Paul Birch started blocking up the orifices that lay before him, he could not get his mind off that work colleague. He knew it would only be a matter of time before something happened between them. He could not help himself. He had to have her.

'Who is she?'

Julie Birch did not beat about the bush. She was sitting opposite her day-dreaming husband at home a few weeks later when she confronted him head on. Julie was a woman led by her instincts and she knew her husband was falling for someone else. She had seen it happen before, in her previous marriage. She was only too well aware of the signs: the distant responses, the late nights at work, the strange phone callers that hung up whenever she answered.

But Paul Birch was not ready to confess. He had only just met this other woman and he was not about to sacrifice eight years of happy marriage for the sake of some passing love interest.

'You bastard. I know there's another woman.'

Julie Birch could not have been more blunt. She was confronting her husband in the hope he would admit it. Then she could give him hell, make him promise not to see her again and maybe, just maybe, they might be able to salvage their marriage.

But Paul Birch was ruining those plans for his wife. After a few years as an astute local politician, he knew that he should never confess unless confronted by incontrovertible evidence. And his hot-tempered wife was going purely on a hunch. It would take more than that to make him tell all.

He did not see the bottle smashing down on the back of his head until it was too late. But Paul Birch certainly felt the searing pain as some splinters of glass embedded themselves in his balding pate. Julie Birch was incensed. This was the ultimate insult. She knew he was seeing someone else but he would not admit it. Now she feared that his affair might develop into something even more long-term. The thought of losing him made Julie even more enraged. She was like a cheetah with a short fuse, ready to strike out at any moment — and that moment had just come.

Paul Birch tried very hard to contain himself in the seconds after his wife's attack. He did not want to respond. He was a master at self-control and now he was facing the ultimate test.

Calmly he got up, walked into the bathroom and started removing the splinters of glass embedded in his skull. Meanwhile, in the hallway outside, she continued a tirade of abuse that was heard at the other end of the street. Those 'good, quiet' neighbours the Birches had suddenly and violently erupted into a couple with problems.

A few minutes later, Paul Birch packed a suitcase in silence as his sobbing wife begged forgiveness and, without a word, walked out of her life, he hoped, forever. It seemed the best course to take. He knew Julie would only get more and more possessive, and he was also concerned about that temper of hers. Its tendency to explode for no good reason was of very great concern to him. But then she considered she had every right to feel angry, and a lot of wives would probably agree.

To say Julie Birch was heartbroken about the break-up of her marriage to Paul would be an understatement. She was devastated. She could not concentrate at work. The flat was in a constant state of chaos. Her whole life revolved around thinking about him every waking minute of the day. Her sense of betrayal was overwhelming. It was as if her whole world had just crashed into nothing. Without Paul, there was no reason to work. No reason to cook. No reason to make love. No reason to live.

She was 45 years old. Her husband had left her. Her kids did not live with her. Julie Birch felt more than just washed up. She was convincing herself that the whole disaster was all her fault. Maybe she had been too possessive. Perhaps she should have handled things differently. But the bottom line was that she was a passionate woman who could not change her ways. She had always been a very upfront, honest sort of person and it was too late to change.

The trouble was that she believed she had brought it all on herself. It was the classic scenario. He had done wrong. He had gone off with another woman. But now, in the cold light of day, she was blaming herself.

Quite simply, the torment was killing her spirit and her appetite for life — and when that happens people start to get desperate.

'Bastard. I'm gonna pour acid over both of you in the street.'

It was a short, sharp message delivered with the hatred that only a scorned woman can muster. The first few threats seemed harmless enough to Paul Birch and his new lover. But at the back of his mind, he kept remembering the things his wife used to say during their time together.

'I'll blast your balls to bits.'

It sent a shiver up his spine. But he tried to push those worrying thoughts into the background as he attempted to get on with his new relationship.

If only he had known that Julie Birch had already bought herself a dress ... to be buried in after she committed the ultimate sacrifice in the name of wedded bliss. If only he had known that she had made out a will specifically to cover the event of her death in violent circumstances. If only he had known just how distraught she had really become.

Julie Birch counted out the money in ten crisp twenty-pound notes before she exchanged pleasantries with the man who sat next to her in a car parked near one of the roughest council estates in Kingston.

Naturally, he re-counted the cash before handing over her purchase — a sawn-off shotgun of the type preferred by Essex-based bank robbers rather than by your everyday jealous wives.

But her underworld contact asked no questions. As far as he was concerned, it was none of his business what she intended to do with that lethal weapon.

Julie Birch wrapped the gun in a piece of cloth and put it in a holdall before getting out of the man's car and heading back to her job at the hairdressing salon. She didn't feel in the least bit bad about what she was about to do. On the contrary, she was already starting to feel relief. Paul would get his just desserts.

Rush-hour on the afternoon of July 16 1987 seemed a fairly ordinary event in Kingston. It was a reasonably hot summer's day and lots of people were out in the town centre in their shirtsleeves, heading home after a hard day at work.

Amongst those commuters was Julie Birch. She had just left the hairdresser's, carrying that same holdall she used to purchase the sawn-off shotgun two days previously. But now that bag contained another item as well: her burial dress.

Julie was excited in a nervous sort of way. At last the big day had come. She had phoned Paul earlier and convinced him to come to the flat in Horace Road to 'discuss a few things'. Paul had been relieved that she sounded so composed, so calm. He had been very worried about her response to him ever since she smashed that bottle over his head a few months earlier. Now perhaps they could discuss the details about their divorce arrangements in a civilised manner. But divorce was the last thing on Julie Birch's mind.

Paul Birch felt a little strange having to knock on the door of his own flat when he turned up just after five that afternoon. After many years of walking the short route to and from work, he had to admit he missed the convenience of living so near to his job. But that was just one of the sacrifices he had made in the name of love.

As his wife opened the door to him, he stood there for a moment, awkward about what to do next. A kiss or similar greeting seemed out of the question when he looked at Julie's face. He could see the tension in her eyes. The feeling of betrayal was clearly lingering within her. He tried to be polite but it was hard to ignore her agitated state. He just prayed that she wouldn't start smashing bottles over his head again.

'Bastard.'

This time, Paul Birch could not fail to see it coming. She had whipped out the sawn-off shotgun more like a Basildon bank robber than a quietly-spoken 45-year-old mother of three. Julie Birch knew exactly where to aim. She was going to make sure that if she could not have him, then no-one else ever would again.

Julie held the stump-like weapon at an angle, with the squat double barrels aimed downwards at his groin, and pulled the trigger without a moment's hesitation. The pellets connected with his thigh, just inches from the spot that his wife was really trying to hit.

'No. No. No. Oh my God.'

The Birches neighbours had heard them argue many times over the previous few months but when they heard those gun shots, even they realised there was something definitely more serious happening this time. The net curtains at the bay windows of all those houses must have been working overtime as resident after resident came to their window to see what those shots were all about.

Inside the flat, the carnage had only just begun ...

Julie Birch was disappointed by her aim. The intention had been to blast his balls to bits. She had always kept her word. It was the least he deserved. But she wanted to keep the other cartridge for herself. So now she would have to use a different method to teach him never to cheat on her again.

She pulled out a knife and looked down at the moaning figure in the living room of that once-cosy love nest where they had shared so many passionate moments. He was looking up at her, his eyes pleading for mercy, in his thigh a bloody wound. But it wasn't enough. And as Paul Birch looked at his wife he must have sensed the horrors that were about to follow.

Julie hitched up her skirt and straddled her husband just the way she had straddled him all those years before when she had taught him so much about making love. But this time her intention was not to have sex with him.

For a few moments she glared down at him, a twisted smirk on her face. She was enjoying his obvious agony. Now it was time to cause some more.

The first time she sank the blade into his chest, she felt the ripping of his flesh as bone hit handle. Her husband gasped for air beneath her, hyperventilating like some desperate asthma sufferer. Julie stopped for a split second — in a weird way it was not that dissimilar from what happened when they had sex together. But his stomach and groin area was where she was aiming her knife. The second plunge of that deadly weapon proved even more lethal. His gut was now ripped open like a plastic bin liner that had been overfilled. His organs were squelching and seeping out through the thin layer of fat.

As four policemen tried to break down the front door to the flat, she inflicted at least three more deadly wounds to the crimson mess of what was once her vibrant, healthy husband.

And when the officers actually managed to burst in, she turned the shotgun on herself as she sat there still straddling her husband in a bizarre, sexually provocative pose — and fired into her heart. Unfortunately, she missed her target that time as well and ended up shooting herself in the shoulder.

The four policemen were astounded by what they found. The bloody, but still just alive, Paul Birch was writhing in agony under the full weight of his shapely, blood-splattered wife. Four-and-a-half hours later, Paul Birch died in Kingston Hospital. Doctors said he bled to death after his wife had punctured his heart during the frenzied knife attack.

In August, 1988, Julie Beulah Birch was committed to a mental hospital for an indefinite period after she admitted the manslaughter of her husband on the grounds of diminished responsibility.

During the trial at Southwark Crown Court, defending counsel Mrs Nemone Lethbridge said: 'She really cannot remember anything after the shot. She had a brainstorm. It was a rotten marriage.'

In a taped interview Julie Birch said: 'I had planned it for some time. Killing Paul to me is like getting rid of a slug. It was the greatest pleasure I have had in my entire life — pulling the trigger.'

The following year, three appeal court judges overruled the Southwark Crown Court judge who sentenced Birch, saying that the doctors at the hospital where she was held — who did not feel she was a general danger to the public — could decide when she was well enough to be released. Today, she is believed to be a free woman.

2

Desperate Measures

The tiny villages scattered around the Yorkshire town of Rotherham consist of tightly-knit communities where absolutely nothing goes unnoticed. The local pub and the corner shop are still the places where residents exchange pleasantries and gossip, just as they have been doing for more than a hundred years.

Coal mining is still the most important source of income in the area. Its influence can be felt throughout the area — from the blackened faces that emerge from the mines after a gruelling day's work to the neat terraces of homes built in Victorian times for the forefathers of those very same miners.

The village of Wath was a classic example. Cobbled streets still remained as a warm reminder of the days when the only means of transport was a pony and trap. Early mornings were, as more often than not, dominated by the damp mist that seemed to descend on the village like a vast blanket, waiting for the heat of the sun to burn it away. At about that time each weekday, the men in those tiny households would emerge for yet another gruelling day down the pits. If they were lucky, they'd get to walk down the street in the company of one of their children, employed to deliver the tabloid newspapers that were often a family's only real link with the outside world.

But by 1984, modern times bad begun to catch up with life in places like Wath. Most families still relied on mining as their main source of income, but there was a disturbing element creeping into the once solid-as-a-rock community — crime. For more years than anyone cared to remember, Wath had been pretty much a crime-free zone. Certainly a few apples were stolen and maybe the odd pint of milk from a doorstep, but nothing more serious than that.

However, the greed and cunning that seemed to come as part of the Margaret Thatcher economic package in the early 1980s was inevitably heading for places like Wath. It might have arrived a few years after most of the rest of the country, but it got there all the same.

That was how PC Pat Durkin found himself transferred to the once non-existent Wath Police Station. Now, it was hardly a hotbed of activity but the very fact that the Yorkshire Constabulary considered it necessary to increase the quota of uniformed officers covering the area was proof in itself. The threat of serious crime had reared its ugly head.

PC Durkin was the sort of police officer every community prays for. With his dark hair and medium-length sideburns, he had a friendly, warm manner that truly endeared him to the community. What made him even more acceptable to them was the fact that he had been a coal miner himself until his mid-twenties.

And to cap matters, when he arrived in Wath, PC Durkin came amid stories of incredible bravery that threatened to turn him into a comic-book style hero overnight.

Back in 1978, he had received an award after rescuing a woman in a coma from a blazing inferno. PC Durkin had kicked open the door of Mrs Barbara Matthewman's smoke-filled flat in Rawmarsh and battled through the dense, choking smoke to try and find her. For many minutes he wandered blindly through the stench and fumes to seek out Mrs Matthewman. Then he grabbed the 25-year-old woman and pulled her to safety.

Afterwards, it emerged that she had been in a diabetic coma and if it had not been for PC Durkin's outstanding courage she would almost certainly have died. Incredibly, the gutsy officer then went back in to the flat once more to help put out the blaze before it spread to any of the nearby homes.

You could certainly say that by the time PC Durkin arrived in Wath his reputation was second to none. Locals welcomed him as one of their own. And he had no intention of shattering their illusions just as long as he walked the beat of their cobbled streets.

She was tall, blonde and very shapely. Her hair flowed like the waves on a choppy ocean. The curls seemed to bounce, as she walked uprightly and confidently. Her eyes were deep and sensuous, always probing beneath the surface like a reptile sizing up its prey. Her hips were wide, but not so big as to put off any likely suitor. They just gave the impression that she was strong in every sense of the word. Capable of taking on whatever any man had to offer.

But then Diana Jade Perry was a very headstrong 25-year-old woman. She enjoyed her work as a clerk in the Department of Health and Social Security office in Wath. Diana felt a certain sense of power because her job at the DHSS gave her a unique insight into the community she lived in. She knew who was out of work or why someone was fired. But best of all she knew which men in the community were just lazy no-hopers trying desperately to avoid a real job at all costs.

Diana also got a thrill out of seeing some of those unemployed men studying her as they queued up for dole money. But then it was hardly surprising that she caused a little stir. Compared to her dowdy workmates, Diana looked like a beauty queen. She tended to dress all in black. One of her favourite outfits was a figure-hugging dress that clung to her like a glove. Rounded off with distinctive five-inch stiletto heels, she really did cut quite a sight in that drab, grey office.

Sometimes she would give some of those men a little flash of thigh as her tight-fitting skirt rode up her legs while she moved position at her desk. She could feel all their eyes feasting upon her and it gave her a very nice sensation. Nothing too sordid, just a tingle in the right places.

But one of the problems with Wath was that it tended to be a very quiet place for an active, lively person like Diana Perry. She increasingly found herself getting more excitement out of those harmless interludes in the office than anything she could do in her own spare time.

She hated the local pubs because they were still very male-orientated places where single, sexy women like Diana were looked upon as intruders into a masculine world of darts and chit-chat about soccer and rugby league. Often she would sit at home in her tiny flat in Church Street, opposite the police station in Wath, and watch those handsome bobbies in their dark blue uniforms going in and out. Then she would settle in front of the television and tune in to her favourite shows like *Coronation Street* and *Crossroads* and try to imagine what life might be like in a more glamorous location.

But as the months progressed, she became increasingly bored with the lack of social opportunities in Wath. At 25, she was almost over the hill in marriage terms. Most women took their wedding vows no later than their early twenties in a place like Wath. Diana was seriously worried that she would never find Mr Right. And then there were the more basic emotions, like feeling the need to have a man sexually. Certainly she had enjoyed a good time with men over the years, but there seemed to be a real lack of available males in Wath. She wanted someone with a little edge. A little daring. Sometimes, she used to fantasise at night about that perfect knight in shining armour who would sweep her off her feet and ravish her and satisfy her every demand.

Diana was starting to spend more and more time watching those good-looking bobbies over the road. Some evenings she would spend ages discreetly peeping through the curtains, trying to work out which one she liked best. Then she would at least go to bed with the features of that handsome face and uniform stamped in her memory. It wasn't the same as the real thing but it would have to do — for the moment.

'I'm sorry to trouble you, but I've gone and locked myself out of my flat over the road. Could you help?'

It was a dream come true for Diana Perry when she found the perfect excuse to turn her fantasies into reality. As she stood pouting slightly in front of PC

Pat Durkin, she knew instantly that he was the one for her.

'No problem. I'll come over and see what I can do.' Pat Durkin could not help giving her an admiring glance as he cast his eyes up and down her body. That tight-fitting black dress really showed off her curves. But there was something familiar about her. He hesitated for a moment and then remembered. A few days earlier, he and a colleague had seen her going into the block of flats opposite.

'That looks like a bit of fun, Pat.'

His colleague had always had an eye for the girls. Now PC Durkin couldn't wait to tell him the next day whose flat he'd been into.

As Diana and her knight in shining armour headed for the exit to the police station, the station sergeant called after him:

'Pat. You take as long as you like, mate.'

Diana Perry knew exactly what the implication was, but she did not care. She already felt that unique tingle of sexual excitement flowing through her body.

PC Pat Durkin also knew that this was going to end up being more than just a plain old boring domestic call. He sensed the moment she walked into the station that something would happen between them. And, as he watched her body clinging ever so tightly to that black dress as they walked up the stairs to the flat, he knew that they would connect.

After all, he was not married any more. His

wife Jenny had long since departed. In fact, it had been a very distressing time for all concerned because she had suffered a fairly nasty nervous breakdown. Luckily for PC Durkin, no one took any notice of Jenny's accusations that he had driven her to insanity because of his insatiable appetite for sex of any description. The doctors said she was suffering from delusions. How could a respectable police officer be committing the sort of sickening sex acts she was accusing him of?

Even when Mrs Durkin tried to make the doctors go to their house to see the weapons of sexual destruction he used on her, they ignored her. The hysterical outbursts. The crazy accusations. They were all indicative of a seriously deluded woman. PC Durkin just stood firm and smiled politely whenever the doctors tried to bring up the subject of his own sexual preferences. Luckily, they were too embarrassed to push the situation.

When Mrs Durkin was committed indefinitely to a mental hospital it seemed the kindest thing to do in the circumstances. PC Durkin quietly and tactfully filed for divorce, and the subject of his first marriage became hidden behind a veil of secrecy that no one dared try to penetrate.

'Poor Pat. He must have had a rough time.'

That was about the nearest anyone ever came to referring to Jenny Durkin. And that was the way PC Durkin planned to keep it.

Back at the front door to Diana Perry's flat that

evening in the winter of 1984, PC Durkin was starting to get those urges again for the first time in years. As he fiddled with the front door lock in a bid to open it for her, he felt his hand shaking with expectation. This might well be the perfect one for him.

Diana saw his hesitancy and took it to mean that Durkin was just as aware of the chemistry between them as she was. Their hands touched as he twisted and turned the lock until the door finally fell open. She had engineered the meeting she so desperately wanted. Now the next stage was to lure him into her life. It would not take long.

The first few occasions they had sex it was warm, romantic and very satisfying. He seemed to be able to switch her on from any one of a hundred different parts of her body. She had lusted after him in an animal fashion. It was the first time in her entire life that the object of her fantasies had become a reality.

She liked to make him keep his well-pressed, dark blue uniform on until the last possible moment. Then she would pull the silver buttons so hard they would pop undone as she searched for his chest and nipples to feast upon.

PC Durkin played along with her happily. He always enjoyed straight sex the first few times with a woman. But he knew there would come a time when he would want to try something different. Always in the back of his mind he was scheming some sick and twisted act.

Meanwhile, two rather lonely people stuck in a

grey, quiet mining community in the middle of Yorkshire were devouring each other with the sort of sexual expertise few would ever experience in a lifetime. They were definitely two lost souls looking for something to break the monotony of life. PC Durkin laughed quietly to himself as he thought of his colleagues working hard at the station across the road, and then turned towards Diana and began kissing her neck uncontrollably.

She returned the passion by pulling his hair so that his head went lower. Then she stuck out her breasts so that he could not avoid licking and sucking them. He enjoyed her forcefulness. He thought it might be a clue to the sort of sex they would eventually enjoy together. But for the moment this would do.

As she pushed him further down below her breasts and past her tummy button, she could feel the burning passion reaching a crescendo. She wanted him to use his tongue as the ultimate weapon of pleasure. This surely must be love and lust wrapped into one, she thought. No one could create such extraordinary sensations and not feel strongly for his partner.

The climax became all the more intense as she lay there thinking about her future with a man whose first wife lay strapped to a bed in a nearby mental hospital.

'Let's move in together.'

Diana Perry had taken the words right out of

her lover's mouth. He had been longing to build up the courage to ask her but now she had beaten him to the line.

'Get your things together and we'll move you in tonight.'

Diana could not quite believe her ears. This really was becoming a dream come true. All the lust and passion of the previous few weeks had brought them both to the same conclusion — for completely different reasons.

PC Durkin — the hero cop with a soft touch — was certain she would do whatever he asked. This time, there would be no nervous breakdowns. No hysterical outbursts at the most crucial moments. Diana had been primed to be his love slave. She was so besotted by him that he was convinced she would do anything. In any case, she was hardly an innocent bystander herself.

She had confessed to the policeman that she had certain sexual desires that he might find offensive. He tried to assure her that as far as he was concerned, 'anything goes'. But Diana Perry's idea of sexual adventure was not in the same league as the man she had just agreed to share a home with.

As she moved all her things into his comfortable, spacious flat nearby in Sivilla Road, Kilnhurst, word soon spread about the 'woman in black''. Neighbours could not help noticing her in her expensive designer outfits that were always only one colour.

Kilnhurst was a similar sort of community to

Wath. The same priorities. The same prejudices. The same bleakness. But PC Durkin was much happier now that he had got her out of that flat opposite the police station in Wath. He wanted to ensure that she was not tempted to wander in the direction of any other bobbies. Her confession that she adored the police uniform he wore made Durkin wonder just how easily she might stray if tempted. Also, he knew he could never carry out the full extent of his sexual obsessions in a flat just a few yards from where his colleagues worked.

But Diana Perry had one hobby that she did not really mention to her policeman lover during the first few lustful weeks of their relationship. Her love of wearing black had a deeper significance because she was fascinated by Nazi regalia and by the workings of the extreme right-wing political organisation, the National Front.

At a time when Britain was in the middle of an immigration crisis that threatened to tear the country apart, Diana considered herself very much a blue-blooded Aryan who disapproved of the hard-working Asians and West Indians who had settled in Yorkshire over the previous twenty years.

To start with, she did not mention her feelings to PC Durkin in case it put a damper on their love affair. But she still continued buying Nazi mementos at a shop in Rotherham. When the time was right, she would show him all her trophies. But for the moment, she was worried that he might get the wrong impression from the jackboots, the helmets and the leather jackets — not to mention the literature that spoke in vivid detail about cleansing the world of all its so-called impurity.

But her obsession with all these trophies from the sickest regime in the history of the world had been growing all the time. A year earlier, she had decided she wanted to start collecting German weapons of destruction. Her first purchase was a 9mm Luger pistol.

On the day she bought it she took it home, unwrapped the packaging and just looked at it for several minutes. Admiring its shape and size, she stroked it gently and felt the coldness of the metal on her fingertips. Some days, she would take it to her lips and kiss the barrel softly and sensuously.

She could not wait for her lover to get home later that evening. She had decided that the time had come to tell him about her fantasies. She pushed the end of that Luger barrel a few inches into her mouth and sucked it hard and let her mind wander forward to the love and passion they would most definitely experience that night.

When PC Pat Durkin got back to his steaming love nest that evening, he got just the sort of surprise he had been longing for. He had refrained from confessing his own sexual obsessions to her, in the hope that he could gradually introduce them to her as their appetite for outrageous lust increased.

Now, his beautiful blonde girlfriend was telling him about her own sexual habits and it was like holding a red rag to a bull. Durkin felt a surge of sexual excitement stream through his body as she told him about her fascination with the Nazis and her substantial collection of memorabilia. He thought he knew then that no amount of sexual force would be too much for her.

As her hand crept up his blue-trousered leg and began probing and squeezing, he felt the rush of adrenalin. This time they would do everything humanly possible in the name of love.

Diana Perry pulled the black leather jackboots up and just over her knees. They were easy to get on over the sheer black stockings, and the three dark shades seemed to compliment her body so perfectly. As his eyes panned up from the black leather to the grey silk to the black cotton of her garter belt, he took a deep breath and absorbed the living fantasy before his very eyes.

'Now bend over.'

PC Durkin did not sound very forceful in his command the first time around. He knew he needed to be stronger. He looked her straight in the eyes and repeated the instruction:

'Bend over *now*!'

Diana Perry had not meant it to end up like this. She had seen her sexual Nazi-style outfit as part of foreplay before a straight sexual encounter. But now her lover was expecting something more. She hesitated for a moment before acknowledging that he obviously meant business. Her love for him was so strong that she decided to let him do whatever he wanted.

She bent over the end of the bed and waited for that first crack of the whip which he held so firmly in his hand.

The first few lashes were not too hard, so she just bit her lip and decided that it would soon be over and then they could both devour each other like they had done so often in the past. But PC Durkin had other ideas on his mind. This was only the beginning.

The next half-dozen lashes were much harder and they left deep weals in her flesh. She tried to get up after each one, but he pushed her down forcefully and told her:

'Don't move or I'll have to punish you even more.'

Diana was scared now. Each slash was more painful than the last and she could hear the trembling of excitement in his voice. She knew that he would not stop until he was satisfied.

Yet, incredibly, her love for him dominated her mind even at that awful moment. She felt as if she had somehow caused the pain by encouraging him to think those evil thoughts. She got sexual excitement out of wearing those outfits, so the natural next stage was to get involved in sadism of some kind. But she did not like being hurt and she was unsure what to think of a man who so dearly wanted to cause so much pain and suffering.

By the time he eventually stopped, the agony

was so great that she was crying real tears of fear. But he did not care. He simply turned her over and forced himself on her. Even then, she kept thinking: 'It's all my fault. It's all my fault.'

As the months went by, Diana Perry got more and more confused by her relationship with PC Pat Durkin. One side of her wanted to feel disgust for him, while the other side admired his daytime persona — that of a loving, trusting servant of law and order. Despite repeated abuse at his hands, she felt somehow that she was getting what she deserved.

She dearly wished she had never dressed up in those Nazi jackboots that first night, but she could not turn the clock back and he was all she had. Now, he forced her to wear the same slinky costumes that she had once so enjoyed putting on to tease and tantalise him.

But his beatings were getting worse and worse. The whips were used virtually every night, and then he would make her do things that she never even dreamt of in her wildest fantasies. Some nights, he would come home armed to the teeth with an assortment of sex aids like vibrators and dildos. And those were the nights when the sex was still relatively gentle. Diana was not a prudish person and she liked experimenting, just so long as it was mutually enjoyable. After all, there was little else to do in Kilnhurst.

The sex aids seemed to divert him from

inflicting pain and suffering, and Diana's unswerving love was starting to take on a much more serious dimension. As the beatings subsided, she began to wonder if perhaps there was a chance they could live happily ever after.

She still had no idea that PC Durkin's first wife was locked up inside a mental hospital after the torture she had suffered at the hands of her brutal husband.

'Come on. Let's do it now.'

For once, this was not PC Pat Durkin demanding that his live-in lover agree to yet more sex. This time, the couple were on a rare outing together in the nearby town of Rotherham. It was mid-November, and the biting gusts of wind blowing off the nearby moors were making her curly hair sweep from her face to reveal its slightly rounded contours.

Durkin knew exactly what Diana was referring to. She was pointing at the Rotherham Registry Office. She wanted him to marry her there and then. That way, neither of them would have any time for regrets. It was all or nothing as far as both of them were concerned, or so Diana hoped.

PC Durkin stopped for a moment on the pavement outside the registry office. He wanted a few seconds to think about what most people consider the most momentous decision of their lives. He thought about them as a couple. They seemed pretty happy. The sex was outstanding. She was a good cook. She seemed besotted by him. What else could a man want out of marriage?

He turned and put his arms around her and kissed her full on the lips as that icy wind blew around their ankles.

'Come on then. Let's get it over and done with, lass.' The registrar was used to slightly more advance notice of a wedding than Diana and Pat were prepared to give him.

'But you need witnesses. I cannot marry you without witnesses.'

Nothing would deter the vibrant couple.

PC Durkin dashed down the steps of the office and spotted two old ladies pulling shopping trollies behind them.

'Excuse me, ladies. Would you mind doing me a very big favour?'

Ten minutes later, Mr and Mrs Durkin emerged from the registry office, complete with wedding certificate and the sort of beaming smiles that usually say it all. It was the most romantic day of Diana's life.

She turned to her loving husband and quietly whispered in his ear: ''Til death us do part ...'

On the way home to Kilnhurst that November day of 1984, Diana truly hoped that marrying PC Durkin would mark a new step towards everlasting happiness. She put all those thoughts of sexual abuse behind her. After all, they had reverted to more traditional ways to excite each other in recent weeks, so she hoped all his sadistic pleasures were now a thing of the past.

Maybe it was an inbuilt naivety on her part, but she was convinced that now they were married he would change into a full-time loving, caring husband rather than the brutal punisher he had shown himself to be earlier in their relationship.

But there was something missing from that wedding ceremony that deeply troubled Diana — a photographer. That night, as they cuddled and kissed romantically on the sofa, at the home that now belonged to both of them, she stopped to ask him:

'What about some photos to mark the event?'

'You arrange it. We'll go to a studio and have them done really nicely.'

Diana was so pleased now. She would have an everlasting memento of her dream marriage to the man of her fantasies.

'I'll wear an extra-special outfit just for the occasion.'

She was already planning a very sexy surprise for the man in her life.

Wedding photographer Tony Munclark had thought he'd seen it all before when Diana and Pat Durkin came excitedly into his studio for a 'very special photo session'. She clutched her new husband's arm, just like they always did straight after a wedding. Sadly, that lovingness was, more often than not, soon forgotten in the midst of the long-term warfare that mostly passed for marriage.

But for the moment, they looked like every happy couple Tony had ever photographed during his career. She had on a smart, well-fitted white skirt and matching jacket that any bride would have been proud of. And PC Durkin wore his best dark suit with a white tie and shirt, just to add that matrimonial feeling to the occasion.

As photographer Tony snapped happily away, he could see through his viewfinder that Diana Durkin was really getting a kick out of having her picture taken. She wrapped one leg around her new husband's hips. Then she twisted and squirmed her own legs together and licked her lips with the tip of her tongue as the shutter kept clicking away.

Every few moments she got more and more daring. Soon she was probing her husband's ear with her tongue, urging the slightly surprised photographer to 'carry on — don't stop'.

The truth was pretty obvious for PC Durkin and that photographer to see. She was getting very turned on by the photo session. But there was still more to come.

'Can you just stop for a second, please.'

The photographer did not mind. He was being paid by the hour and, in any case, this was certainly turning out to be slightly more interesting than your average set of wedding pictures.

But even he was surprised when Diana unzipped her skirt before wriggling it down to the ground. Then she undid the buttons on her blouse and took that off as well.

Both men were stunned. But Diana was not finished yet. Now wearing just a smooth white basque complete with garters and sheer white stockings, she yelled a command at the bewildered Tony:

'Right. Off you go — I want some really steamy pictures to remember this day by.'

PC Pat Durkin was delighted, if a bit stunned, by his brand new wife's extraordinary display of exhibitionism. As she put both her arms around him and nudged her knee into his groin ever so gently, he could not help feeling sexually charged. He was definitely looking forward to getting home that night.

By doing that very public strip, she had convinced PC Durkin that she was game for anything — and in his language that meant a whole assortment of sexual perversions.

The truth was that Diana was always trying desperately to get attention. Her jackboots, her sexy outfits and her strip at the wedding photographer's were all signs of her neverending efforts to please him, to make him happy. But if she had realised that she was simply convincing him that she would perform any sexual act in the name of her love for him, then she would never have done any of those things in the first place.

Meanwhile, PC Durkin's sick and twisted mind was planning a new series of torments for his brand new bride …

Diana Durkin was petrified. Her husband had just wrapped a leather gag around her face and she was having trouble breathing. She kept thinking back to the wedding, the photographs, the happiness. Now, just a few hours after all that, she was being submitted to the sort of degrading act she thought she had married him to escape from.

PC Durkin's idea of sexual fun was to punish his partner in every way he could think of. Maybe it was all those years of working in the police force and keeping his cool in the face of so much danger that did it. Perhaps he had repressed his anger and hatred towards women for so long that it had to get out eventually.

Whatever the reason, Durkin was only concerned with one thing as he tied his wife's arms tightly behind her back — his own self-gratification. This was just the beginning of his sexual merry-go-round. He fully intended to take his wife to the edge of sadism at its very worst. And then he had other plans as well ...

Diana Durkin was stifling the tears because she knew he would pull the ropes even tighter if he heard her crying. She just wished she had never married him. This was living hell and there was no way of escape.

As she felt his hands smashing across her head and back, she tried to console herself with the thought that perhaps she had brought it on herself. She would do anything for him within the normally acceptable bounds of sexual foreplay, but this was too horrible to contemplate.

When it was over, he untied the gag. It was covered in her saliva where she had bitten right through it in a vain bid to avoid the pain that was searing her body. He did not utter a word to her. It was just remotely possible that his own climax had left him feeling just a bit guilty for the outrageous acts he had committed. But then again, his face showed no remorse.

Diana Durkin cried herself to sleep that night. Her mind was just a jumble of confusion. The emotional highs of the wedding had been completely destroyed by the sick and twisted acts he had performed on her. She needed time to think about the future. How was she going to escape?

The next day at work, even her colleagues noticed that she was not the same happy, vibrant, sexy Diana of old.

'That's what marriage does to you, Di,' said one tactless work pal. If only he had known just how close to the truth he really was.

The only thing that remained the same about Diana that day were her clothes — she still wore her traditional black tight-fitting dress, but now she was not capable of flirting with the clients or showing off a little bit of thigh like before. He had destroyed all that. She would never openly display her sexuality again. He had punished her for being so uninhibited. She had learnt her lesson.

Diana dreaded getting home each night in the days following the wedding. Her husband — the man whom she had thought she loved enough to marry less than a week earlier — had become a morose

monster whose only conversation consisted of orders
like:

'Take your clothes off.'

'Bend over.'

'Do as I tell you.'

She kept wishing she had never worn those
Nazi jackboots or the other sexy outfits, then he
might not have presumed he could abuse her the
way he was now intent on doing each and every
evening.

But PC Pat Durkin felt no guilt. Every day at
work he let his mind wander to what he had
planned for that evening's 'entertainment' with his
wife. Like a heroin addict looking for a bigger and
bigger fix, PC Durkin needed to make each act even
more outrageous than the one before. Hours of his
working day were taken up with thinking them
through, planning them down to the last intricate
detail. That was part of the thrill for him. In fact, he
felt almost as excited when he thought through his
sadistic pleasures as when it all actually happened.

Yet Diana Durkin somehow persevered with her
husband. Something inside her made her believe
that she could mend their relationship. There was
still hope, despite the pain and suffering.

That eternal optimism was part of her character.
It was the same ingredient that had created a bubbly,
extrovert persona that PC Durkin had mistaken for a
love of perverted sex.

But on the fifth night of their married life
together, the sick and twisted mind of the deviant

bobby took on a whole new dimension. Not even the ever-tolerant Diana could stand the thought of what her husband proposed.

She looked down at the growling Alsatian and refused point-blank to move until he had taken the animal out of their bedroom. It was at that point she knew that her marriage had truly been made in hell.

The following evening, conversation between husband and wife was virtually non-existent. PC Durkin was still sulking from what he saw as her refusal to co-operate in his sickly bid for sexual gratification.

Diana Durkin was too afraid to talk to him in case he beat her, as he had done pretty regularly in the past. She kept asking herself why she had even married this monster who hid behind the veneer of respectability through his career as a policeman.

As she watched him pour himself his seventh glass of straight whisky that night, she wondered how much longer she could live in that awful place.

'I'm goin' to bed.'

She prayed that he would not follow. She somehow hoped he would stay behind in the kitchen and drink himself into oblivion before collapsing on the sofa. But that was purely wishful thinking on her part.

Within minutes of her pulling the covers tightly over herself he appeared, swaying with the drink and blowing booze-sodden fumes all around the room. She tried to pull the blanket even closer but he yanked it away viciously. She lay there, exposed to his drunken eyes, like a pervert's feast laid out and ready to eat.

She knew this time she would not be able to take any more of his abuse. Her tolerance level was at an all-time low. She shut her eyes tightly and prayed that sleep would take over before anything more could occur.

'Get out, you bitch. Get out.'

Diana did not move at first. She was scared she might incite him further so she lay like a stone on the bed.

'You heard me. Get out.'

She wished that she could just fall asleep. Even her worst nightmares were not as bad as the reality she faced that evening. But PC Durkin had not finished.

She sensed him lunging towards her, so she moved out of the bed speedily and wrapped a dressing gown around herself. She looked around to see his drunken body collapsed on the bed, so she headed towards the kitchen to wait a few minutes for him to be safely asleep.

By the time she crept back into the bedroom he looked truly sound asleep. She lay down on the edge of the bed and pulled the covers over herself very gently so as not to disturb the monster.

It must have been way past midnight by the time she actually got to sleep. Her dreams were just as pleasant as she had hoped for.

'Come on, bitch. Do it.'

Dawn was just peeping through the curtains when Diana opened her eyes to that familiar aggressive tone she had come to loathe so much. Her husband — the gentle policeman so adored by the community — was trying to molest her as she lay next to him. She pushed him away roughly, but regretted it almost immediately.

She should have known better. He never slept past dawn when he had been drinking heavily. Why on earth did she return to that bed in the first place? Maybe she just thought there was a small chance she might wake up the next morning and he would be a changed man. The truth was that he would never change.

'Get out then.'

PC Durkin gave his bride of just seven days two choices.

'If you don't want to do it, get out. Why d'you come back in here in the first place?'

Diana Durkin clenched her fists with anger. The fear she usually felt had been replaced by a deep-set fury. She had taken just about enough. She got up from the bed and headed for the wardrobe in silence.

PC Durkin was still in an alcoholic haze and took little notice of her as she searched through the wardrobe for something. He just taunted her over and over.

'You're useless. I don't know why I even married you. You're only good for one thing.'

If he had bothered to look up at that moment,

he might have seen the German Luger pointing straight at him. She wished he would watch her, then he would see the end just before it came. That would make the killing even more satisfying. She wanted him to know it was her, then he might realise why.

But PC Pat Durkin lay there as if he did not have a care in the world. All his cruelty to his first wife and now his second was about to catch up with him in a deadly fashion.

She pointed the gun towards his head and squeezed as tight as she could. The muscles on her index finger strained with the tension, but there was nothing she could do to stop it now. The gun jerked downwards slightly in her hand.

The bullet entered his throat and pierced a one-inch hole right through his neck. It was enough to end his abuse for ever.

Next door, neighbour Ferenc Pinter had just got up, when he heard a noise like nothing else he had ever experienced in his lifetime.

'I heard a cry, a death cry. Then all went quiet.'

In July, 1985, Diana Durkin was put on probation for three years for killing her 36-year-old husband. Her plea of guilty to manslaughter on the grounds of provocation and diminished responsibility was accepted by the judge Mr Justice Hodgson, at Sheffield Crown Court.

The judge told the court: 'She poses no danger to anyone.' He also said she had been subjected to 'sadistic behaviour over a long period'.

One of the conditions of Diana Durkin's probation was that she become an in-patient at a psychiatric hospital in Bradford, Yorkshire. PC Durkin's first wife Jenny is believed to still be a psychiatric patient in another mental home.

3

Animal Farm

The Modin farmyard was like something out of another century. The run-down main house looked as if a group of hillbillies had long since abandoned it to the ravages of wild animals. Many of the windows were broken or simply non-existent, their frames hanging limply from hinges, primed for firewood and little else. Step on the porch and your foot would likely plunge through rotten wood. The roof, too, had seen better days. Its flimsy tiles had been ripped off in the furious storms that tumbled down the mountains and across the plains every winter.

Dogs and horses roamed freely in and out of the house and all the surrounding barns as if they owned the place. Every now and again a dog would rummage through the piles of rotting rubbish that leant against the outhouses. The starving animals would devour anything that might pass as food — some decaying piece of fly-infested meat perhaps, or an old tin that might have just a morsel still in it.

The place was covered in shit. Hundreds and hundreds of piles, dotted around the yard like little ant hills. They had long since turned hard in the summer heat but it was difficult to avoid stepping on them as you tried to make your way across the yard to the main house.

To an outsider the Modin farm really did look like the ultimate Orwellian nightmare. A dilapidated, uninhabited place that had long since been deserted by humans. The locals even nicknamed it 'Animal Farm'. It was only the sign at the rotting gate that gave any clue to the fact that somehow one human being still lived there:

STALLIONS AND GUARD DOGS,
PLEASE STAY IN THE CAR.
IF AT HOME, WE WILL COME TO GATE.
THANKS.

Betty Modin was determined to cut herself off from the outside world as much as possible. The animals were her protectors now. She talked to them, fed them (when she had the funds) and loved them in her own strange way.

In fact, she looked like a wild animal herself.

Her thick grey hair, matted in clumps that stuck to her scalp and clothes, which couldn't have been washed since they had been bought, made it quite clear where her priorities lay. Fashion had long since passed her by. But then, at 60 years of age, she had no interest in anything other than her dearly beloved animals. She often used to say that in a perfect world she would never have to speak to a human again as long as she lived.

Some believed she was driven into her bizarre life in the Canadian wilderness by the pain and anguish of an unhappy marriage. It had closed her off, until she had secured for herself a private world of her own which she could cope with. In order to survive, however, she had to put up with the very man she hated and despised so much — her husband Norman.

In 1977 they had finally agreed to separate. Norman could no longer stand her temper tantrums and her weird ideals. She had taken little interest in the upbringing of their children. She rarely spoke to them kindly. Instead, she would shout and rant at Norman and then retreat into her little imaginary world where humans played but a tiny role.

Yet the most vivid memory Betty Modin's children had of their mother was when she brutally killed some of the very animals she adored so much. One of her daughters never forgot how Betty made her tie a dog to a fence and then shot the animal in cold blood because it had killed two ducks. She'd done it there and then, in front of a girl who was only 11 at the time. It was a memory that would haunt the daughter for the rest of her life.

When Betty and Norman split up it was a relief for the whole family. Gentle Norman could not wait to get away from his selfish wife and start a new life on the other side of the country. But he still accepted that he would have to provide for Betty and promised to pay her $1,100 a month to keep herself and her animals in the manner to which they had become accustomed.

But the marriage break-up simply provided Betty with the perfect opportunity to escape from reality forever. With just enough cash each month to keep things going single-handedly, she sank into a timeless existence. Just so long as that cheque came through the post each month, she could keep her animals — and that was all that counted. Her dog food bill alone came to $500 a month. That was, when she remembered to buy it. But then Betty did not care about the state of the farm. Her life was now so interlocked with her darlings that their survival meant her survival. Who cared about bricks and mortar?

When, on October 6 1981, husband Norman turned up for a rare visit to the Canadian wilderness, Betty was not exactly surprised. She had sensed a note of edginess in her estranged husband recently when they spoke on the phone or exchanged letters. She genuinely feared that his visit might have been prompted by a decision to cut off the monthly payments that made her strange lifestyle possible.

Betty may have preferred the company of animals, but she was still a quick-witted, intelligent woman when she wanted to be. In fact, it was her razor-sharp perception of life that probably made her such a loner. She neither trusted nor particularly liked human beings — it was as simple as that.

And now the man she had referred to as 'it' for most of their married life was making a highly suspicious visit to her run-down home. She knew 'it' was hardly likely to be making the long trek to profess his love for her. Love was just a distant memory. Betty wasn't sure whether it had ever existed at all.

Though 61, Norman Modin had enjoyed a whole new lease of life the moment he had left Betty. It took their separation for him to realise just how much of life he had missed out on. His new world consisted of a responsible job as an aircraft mechanic and a comfortable home in the picturesque town of Fort Nelson in British Columbia.

The last thing he wanted to do was visit the rotting ruin of a house that Betty clung to. He had been dreading the journey for weeks, but he steeled himself. It had to be done. It was high time they discussed the money he had willingly been shelling out for the previous four years. Now all the kids were grown up, he believed it was right to divorce and cut down on those crippling payments that were biting into his monthly salary.

As Norman arrived at the huge Edmonton International Airport, he promised himself it would be as brief a visit as possible. He truly hated staying at the farm. She had allowed it to become such a dreadful, unhygienic place that he had refused to sleep in the main farmhouse on the previous couple of visits. Now, he came well prepared for a cold but relatively clean night sleeping in his hire car in one of the outhouses.

It was for that reason he had chosen a 1980 blue and grey Mercury Lynx rental as his cosy home for the next twenty-four hours. At least the pristine vehicle with its comfortable cloth interior would provide him with some escape from the disgusting place his wife called home.

As Norman Modin drove the two-hour journey to his wife's residence, he tuned in the radio to a news station and listened intently to the shock event of that day — the assassination of Egyptian president Anwar Sadat. It was a momentous time in Middle Eastern politics, and many feared that the death of the peace-loving statesman might spark a bloody conflict in the world's most volatile region. US warships stood by nervously, Israel's sabre rattled and the world took a deep breath.

Norman Modin probably felt just as concerned as millions of other North Americans as he journeyed across the barren flatlands. But October 6, 1981 was going to end up being the most significant date in his life for an entirely different reason.

'Betty. We must talk.'

Betty Modin knew the moment she heard the tone of her husband's voice that trouble was brewing. They might have loathed each other for much of their married life together, but she still knew Norman inside out. That was one of the reasons she grew so contemptuous of him. She could always tell what he was going to say before he even got half-way through his stumbling sentences. As far as she was concerned, he was an old bore and the less she had to talk to him the better.

As she sat in the dusty armchair that had once been the family's pride and joy, she considered how to solve the problem at hand. Her husband sat opposite her in another seat that had been badly ravaged by some of the ill-trained dogs that were constantly flowing through that front room like an army of protectors around the short-tempered, eccentric Betty.

'I cannot afford to keep paying you all this money each month.'

Norman was nervous about telling her. He had been dreading this moment for weeks, but at least he was finally tackling the situation head on.

Betty did not reply. She just looked at him through glasses that were perched on the end of her beak-like nose.

'Well. How much can we cut it down to, Betty?'

Norman had started, so he was not about to retreat. It had to be done. He had to sort it all out.

But Betty's mind was working overtime. She was infuriated. Yet again her husband had proved to be such a bloody predictable bastard. How dare he try and cut off her money? Without it, the animals would starve. She did not care about herself, but they were her pride and joy and no one was going to take her 'children' from her.

Betty was not even going to allow him the pleasure of a reply. She reckoned there were other ways to ensure the money continued flowing through.

Norman Modin was concerned by Betty's apparently meek acceptance. He took her refusal to talk about it as an agreement that he should cut down the monthly payments considerably. He continued on his mission:

'How about $500 a month? Surely that would see you through pretty comfortably?'

Still Betty sat there in silence. Why should she degrade herself by even commenting on his outrageous proposition? He never did care anything about the animals she had so cherished. Years earlier he had given her the choice: save her marriage or stay with the animals. Betty Modin said she had no choice at that time, and it was the same now as they tried to 'talk things through'. How could he sit there in her house, watching all her little 'children' playing in the living room, without realising that nothing would persuade her to sacrifice the ones she loved?

Outside, a horse galloped past the window.

Betty Modin decided there and then that nothing would get in her way.

Norman Modin left her, without getting a reply, and trotted off to the barn where his rental car and sleeping bag awaited him. So she wouldn't speak. Let the old bat have her moment of glory. At least he had told her. She couldn't claim later that he had not given her a chance to air her opinions.

The night air was silent for once. So deathly quiet that the only noise was the distant patter of some of the dogs walking across the yard. Then, in the distance, the whirr of a single-prop aircraft — probably a farmer late home from an errand — flying across the canyon a few miles to the east.

On the porch, at least twenty dogs slept peacefully. Every now and again one of them would scratch its stomach as a fat, sleepy fruit fly landed on its coat. Away from the house, the darkness was complete. No shadows. No figures. No light. Just a sea of black permeating the entire countryside. The barn where Norman Modin snored in his rental car was just a few yards away from the main house. He felt quite safe and snug there — it was certainly an improvement on the flea-infested mattresses that he had once suffered in the name of marital bliss.

When the huge, high door to that barn slowly creaked open, Norman was already at peace with the world. Probably dreaming about some distant paradise where there were no dogs, no horses and no Betty Modin. He did not even stir when some of the dogs followed the old woman in. Outside, a gentle breeze had picked up over the barren pastures. It rustled around Betty Modin's ankles for a few moments as she crept slowly and silently over the straw-covered floor. The pitter-patter of her dogs' paws on the same surface sounded like rain coming through the gaping holes in the roof.

A beacon of light suddenly appeared as Betty Modin switched on her small hand-torch and shone it down on the ground before panning it up to the door handle of the Mercury Lynx. She stood there for a moment, thinking. Then one of her dogs rubbed itself against her leg and she remembered why she was there. They were more important to her than anything else in the world. No one was going to take them away.

A slight smile came to her lips as she examined the car door by torchlight. It was unlocked. Perfect.

She stood absolutely still for a moment and waited again. Then she heard it. A slow, sniffling snore. She did not want to shine her torch right in at him until the last possible moment, but she had to make sure he was asleep. For the first time in her life, that snoring sound was reassuring. She had endured so many years of his snorting sleeping habits with a faint disgust. But now she was delighted he made so much noise because it was encouraging her to prepare for a triumphant moment in her life.

Her hand grasped the door handle tightly and she clicked it up. It was such a modern model that the door opened with ease. Her torchlight still shone on the floor, guiding her. She cast the beam across his shoes protruding from the bottom of his sleeping bag. He looked snug covered up like that. For a split second she let the light wander over his craggy face. She would not miss him.

Now was the time. Now he would pay the price for trying to destroy her little kingdom at 'Animal Farm'.

Betty Modin had handled guns since she was eleven years old, so she did not exactly struggle with the shotgun in her right hand. Standing in a cold, precise stance, she held the wooden end tight against her shoulder and aimed at his body, still sleeping soundly just two feet away.

The blast of shot sounded more like a loud thud than a gun firing. The 250-odd pieces of shot pierced that quilted sleeping bag like a rainstorm of metal fragments. Betty watched as he came to — in shock. She shone her torch right in his eyes. She wanted to see the fear in his eyes. He tried to move, in a desperate bid to stop her firing any further shots. But his thigh had been torn to shreds by the force of the blast. In any case, Betty Modin had no intention of firing any more. She wanted to leave him to die a slow and anguished death. He was not going to enjoy the luxury of a quick, sudden execution. In her mind, he deserved the worst type of punishment imaginable.

Three of her dogs leapt up and started to sniff and lick at the gaping wound. One of them chomped up a tattered piece of flesh lying beside him. A good meal. And there might be more yet. Betty left without a word, calling the dogs away as if she were out on a quiet walk in the countryside.

She felt no remorse. Just relief that she had finally done it. The payments would continue on his standing order. She had already decided that as far as the rest of the world was concerned, her husband had disappeared without trace. By morning he would be no more.

Norman Modin fell into a deep coma within seconds of his wife leaving the dingy barn. He was losing blood at an alarming rate and he simply could not fight the fatigue that had overwhelmed his body. He never recovered consciousness and about two hours later, he died through loss of blood.

The next day, Betty did not even bother to go into the barn to see whether her dying husband had somehow managed to crawl out of his crypt. She knew he would be going no place ever again.

She got out a hammer and some splintered wood from across the yard and nailed the doors closed. She had no intention of ever going into that outhouse again. She had achieved what she set out to do — and that was all that mattered.

As the weeks passed and the police came and went, Betty staved off everyone with great skill. She got to quite enjoy telling her story of how her husband never actually turned up to see her on that day in October as he had promised.

She said it was typical of her hard-drinking, estranged, bully of a husband. She reckoned he had probably headed down to Los Angeles.

'It's the sort of place he would like because he is one of 'those'.' She said it in such whispered tones that the policeman interviewing her did not have the faintest idea what she was on about at first.

'Excuse me, Mrs Modin, but what is one of "those"?'

'You know,' she hesitated for a moment. It hurt her even to refer to them by name. 'A homosexual.'

The cop nodded his head understandingly. He would have dearly loved to put her story to the test by searching every inch of that disgusting flea-ridden, rundown farm. There was something about her that he did not trust. Maybe it was the cold stare or the unemotional response each time he talked to her about her recently departed husband.

But there was no actual evidence to link Betty Modin to her husband's mysterious disappearance. Not a shred of proof that she was the person who might be responsible for his vanishing act. For that reason the officer could not even obtain a search warrant to turn the place upside down.

Just a few feet away, the corpse of Norman Modin was gradually being devoured by the insects and rodents that had inhabited that barn for far longer than him.

Betty Modin tried not to give her husband much thought after the dust settled and the inquiries as to his whereabouts ceased. She was just delighted to be able to get on with her sole ambition in life — to raise her 'children' in a safe, happy environment. As the months passed, she continued receiving her husband's cheques — thanks to his standing order and the blank cheques she took from the case he had left in the living room before his death. Betty would forge his signature and then send them to his bank account in British Columbia so that the account he set up for her would continue to be healthy for some years to come. Luckily for her, Norman had been a good saver and, at the rate of $1,100 a month, she knew he had sufficient funds to keep her going well into old age.

And, for some unknown reason, the police investigating the disappearance of Norman Modin never thought to check his bank accounts until many years later.

Over the next few years, Betty never once felt tempted to look inside that barn at the once-gleaming car which her husband had hired. If she had, she would have seen that the cruel, harsh winters had proven beyond doubt that the ability of the Mercury to resist long-term rusting was non-existent. But that was hardly her concern. She was more preoccupied with running the farm and keeping all those animals happy.

Her two daughters were shocked, but hardly surprised, when they occasionally visited their mother. The buildings were getting even more rundown and the plastic rubbish bags were now piled high against a wall around the back of that very same barn where her husband lay entombed. Many of the bags had gashes in them where the dogs had ripped them open in a desperate bid to find a source of food.

Yet her daughters found her as mentally alert as ever. It was as if the disgusting state of her home was completely unrelated to her ability to think and act quickly. Her clothes may have been drab and filthy but her mind was sharp.

One day she held a completely coherent, topical conversation with one of her daughters for two hours on the subject of American politics. She hardly ever read a newspaper and only occasionally listened to the radio, but she seemed to know everything that was going on.

'Bush is just not strong enough. He needs more edge.'

Her daughter looked around at the filthy hovel her mother called home and wondered how on earth she had ever survived such an eccentric upbringing. She thanked God she had managed to escape.

Almost nine years later — in September 1990 — police sergeants Del Huget and Joseph Zubkowski decided they would re-open the file on missing Norman Modin and do one last bit of detective work to see if they could solve the disappearance that had troubled a good few of their predecessors.

When they uncovered the fact that no one had

bothered to investigate Norman Modin's financial status, they started one last digging operation and soon discovered that someone had been forging cheques in his name and that Betty Modin was still receiving her monthly payments.

Once again the finger of suspicion pointed at Betty, now a spritely 70-year-old. But those forged cheques were not enough evidence in themselves to persuade a judge to issue a search warrant. So officers Huget and Zubkowski decided to pay the eccentric lady a visit.

Betty Modin was a bit taken aback when the two policemen called at her home on September 4 1990. It had been many years since her last visit from the law and she had actually presumed that the whole matter was now dead and buried.

The officers seemed friendly enough, but she was very concerned as to why they should come back to her after such a long time. Betty repeated her allegations that Norman Modin was a homosexual who had probably fled to Los Angeles, and tried to cut short the two detectives' visit by claiming she had to feed the horses.

But before she could persuade them to leave they asked her one last question.

'When was the last day you saw your husband, Mrs Modin?'

A long period of time had elapsed since the last time she had been asked that question by the police. She hesitated. Then it came to her.

'It was the day of Anwar Sadat's assassination. I remember hearing it on the radio.'

The officers shook their heads and made a note of Betty Modin's reply without even realising the significance of it. They departed for Edmonton just a few minutes later, none the wiser in the mystery of Norman Modin's disappearance.

Back at the police precinct, Huget and Zubkowski were just going through the motions of putting the case to bed forever, when Huget checked through Betty Modin's original statement to police back in 1981.

Then he spotted it. Betty had clearly claimed that she never even saw her husband on that fateful day of the Sadat killing. She had always stuck steadfastly to her story that he had never shown up to stay at the farm that day. Now, the police had evidence that she was lying. It was enough to get an immediate search warrant issued and within hours they had returned to the filthy farmhouse that was home to countless animals and the very weird Betty Modin.

The huge doors of that barn took quite an effort to open. But, thanks mainly to a thick metal jack, the two officers managed to prise them apart after a few minutes.

Betty Modin stood on the porch as they forced their way in. The officers' eyes panned around the dusty, insect-filled air, which was illuminated by the strong sunlight penetrating every corner of the barn. The unmistakably poignant stench of decaying flesh overwhelmed them.

The two men looked at each other for a moment and then headed towards the rusting remains of the Mercury. The car was covered in a tapestry of cobwebs broken only by the infestation of maggots and mouse droppings that adorned much of the bodywork.

Huget glanced down at the mice scurrying away from the underneath of the car and gasped as a sweet, sickly odour threatened to gag him. It hung thick in the air and caught in his throat so that he had to swallow to avoid choking. He found himself clearing his throat again and again.

His partner Zubkowski stood back in silence. Both men knew what they were about to find but they were trying to delay the awful moment for as long as possible.

Huget gingerly opened the door. Trying to avoid the crust of insects, he pulled carefully at the handle. But it did not move. He was dreading the moment, but unless he actually pulled that door open with some real force it would not budge. Ten years of inactivity had done more than just rust a few hinges.

He drew a deep breath and pulled with all his strength. The door eased open slowly and there, on the back seat was the partial mummified body of Norman Modin. They had built themselves up into such a state of anxious expectation that the reality of the situation was not quite so horrendous. It looked more like something from a horror movie set than an actual corpse.

At first, they both tried to avoid looking at his face. Their eyes started at his feet, still covered in the leather shoes he had put on for that last fateful journey from his home in British Columbia. They were peeping out rigidly from the bottom of the sleeping bag — almost as if they were unconnected to the grotesque head that slumped limply to one side, with a yellow cap perched precariously at an angle.

One side of the face had been eaten down to the bone by the armies of termites that had feasted on his remains for ten long years. But the other side of his face was still remarkably intact because he had slumped against the side of the sleeping bag and the insects had not been able to penetrate that part of his head.

Huget and Zubkowski both swallowed hard as they examined the remains of Norman Modin in absolute silence. Suddenly, Huget felt something wet and moist at his ankle. He was startled and jumped back a few inches before realising that one of Betty Modin's dogs was sniffing at his feet. Then another three came barging into the barn and tried to break past the two policemen blocking the way to the car.

The dogs were like hungry savages, having smelt the congealed and rotting remains of the man who was once their master. Huget and Zubkowski struggled to hold back the dogs and slammed the car door shut to stop them getting to the corpse.

Out on the porch, Betty Modin felt relieved. That dark and disturbing secret had remained locked inside her mind for longer than any human could be expected to tolerate. Now, at least, the fear of her husband being discovered was no more.

But her only concern as the two detectives read Betty Modin her rights was her animals. She knew they would never survive without all her loving care and attention.

On December 6 1991, Betty Modin stood emotionless as Justice Alex Murray found her guilty of the manslaughter of her husband. Six weeks later, the 71-year-old widow was sentenced to four years in jail after the same judge told her: 'I consider the degree of culpability on your part to be of a high order. In fixing sentence, this court must consider the fact that such behaviour is unacceptable and therefore repudiated by society.'

Modin was also ordered never to touch any firearm again. Justice Murray also ordered that her term be served in a facility near Edmonton where medical service was readily available as her health had seriously declined after her arrest and she was in need of a hip replacement operation, as well as suffering from severe arthritis.

4

Possessed!

She was a tall, shapely blonde with smooth bobbed hair and wide, brilliant blue eyes. Her hips were generous but well in proportion with the rest of her body, giving an impression of strength and capability; well able to deal with anything that life might throw at her. But then twenty-eight-year-old Tracey Gaywood was a very intimidating woman. She threw herself into her work as a well-paid market researcher with great enthusiasm but she always seemed to be on the edge of sadness, never quite able to sustain her success. She had similar problems in her social life. So, when she met Jeremy Parkins in 1990, she truly believed that she might have found a perfect partner. He was generous, gentle and loving, and she felt he wanted to learn as much from her as she did from him.

For five months Tracey and Jeremy enjoyed such a sexually active relationship that Tracey became convinced it was leading to even greater things, like love and marriage. Tracey really enjoyed using her body to please Jeremy. It wasn't a dirty, salacious thing to do. She saw it as deeply romantic and she liked to ensure he wanted her every night. She also knew full well that regular love making was a sure way to hold on to your man.

Jeremy — a softly-spoken twenty-nine-year-old — was completely swept off his feet at first. Tracey was the first woman he had ever met who actually enjoyed sex and was genuinely passionate. She taught him many things about the art of love and their relationship appeared to their families and friends to be safe and secure.

However, after those first months of passion began to fade, conversation between the two became a little more awkward. As the love making subsided, so did their ability to connect. Then Tracey revealed to Jeremy that she had suffered from a weight problem in the past and she also disclosed to him that she had become dangerously addicted to slimming pills when she was a little younger.

Jeremy did not take much notice until his lover started to 'act weirdly' whenever they went out together. She would twitch uncontrollably and then burst into tears. It got progressively more serious. She began talking openly of a 'demon' that haunted her. Jeremy was bemused by her claims but they definitely left him feeling a little uneasy about their relationship. Perhaps if he had been a more demonstrative fellow he might have got her to see someone to discuss her 'problem'.

In fact, Jeremy actually thought Tracey's problems were caused solely by those slimming pills. However, as the weeks turned into months it became clear that Tracey had much more serious anxieties.

One day an envelope from Tracey arrived at Jeremy's home. He recognised the writing and opened it to find a series of poems written in scraggy, erratic hand writing. The wording of the poems was disturbing, to say the least. Tracey referred to the sort of sexual acts she wanted Jeremy to perform. She seemed to be interpreting their relationship in a completely different way from Jeremy. If Tracey's intention was to improve the sexual side of their romance, then she had picked the wrong man in Jeremy. Her demands made his hair stand on end. He was starting to wonder how he had got himself involved with such a strange woman.

Soon alarm bells were ringing loud and clear in Jeremy's head. He read the poems a second time and concluded that they had to come from a very sick mind. It was time to end the relationship before it got any more serious.

It also has to be pointed out that Jeremy's departure was partly influenced by his meeting Linda Willis, a straight-talking, sane, twenty-seven-year-old brunette who seemed like a breath of fresh air compared with Tracey. Linda was as sensible as Tracey was bizarre. She instantly provided Jeremy with a more secure basis upon which to have a relationship.

Jeremy — ever considerate — decided to remove Tracey from his life slowly and tactfully. He sensed that she might go completely mad if he just dropped her like a stone, so he set about gently extracting himself from her life. The warning signs of fatal attraction problems kept on appearing. He needed to tread carefully, warned some of his friends.

Eventually, Tracey seemed to accept that she could not have Jeremy to herself. He had very tactfully eased himself away from her and soon they were seeing each other only very occasionally, although Jeremy did not cut the tie completely, just in case she cracked up.

What Jeremy did not realise was that Tracey was seething with anger about being dropped by him. She was thankful for seeing him every now and again but she still wanted him all to herself and she was determined not to let him off the hook that easily.

Besides becoming increasingly obsessed with Jeremy, Tracey was also in desperate need of a regular bed partner and the occasional meeting with Jeremy was not enough to satisfy her sexual demands, especially since that side of their relationship had all but disappeared. As the split between them grew more apparent, so did Tracey's determination to have Jeremy entirely to herself.

Tracey would become particularly angry on the evenings when she found herself alone in her small flat, knowing that Jeremy was probably out with *her*. She could not help thinking about what she was missing and it fuelled her burning desire to get him back.

It was during those lonely evenings in front of the television that she started writing the most vicious, perverted poison-pen letters to Jeremy. In her mind she felt she had been betrayed by him for another woman and she wanted him back. Somehow, she convinced herself that if she promised to perform those shocking acts then he might feel he could not resist her.

When Jeremy received the letters he was even more shocked than when he got the poems a few months earlier. It wasn't just the sexual activity described that stunned Jeremy. In one letter Tracey talked about killing Linda in order to win Jeremy back. It sent a shiver up his spine.

In another letter she wrote explicit details of the sexual acts she wanted to perform with Jeremy. There was mention of bondage, rubber and leather. Unfortunately, none of it appealed to Jeremy in the slightest. Tracey seemed to be living out her weird fantasies through her letter writing. She referred to other highly explicit sex acts and they continually culminated in the death of Linda.

In her increasingly deranged and jealous mind,

Tracey believed that by promising Jeremy totally uninhibited sex she could win him back. Her promise to kill Linda for him was just the icing on the cake.

Then, in January 1992, more than a year after his split with Tracey, Jeremy and Linda had a row and Linda walked out on him to stay with a friend.

For some reason, Jeremy then made a very serious error. He called Tracey up and asked if he could spend the night at her home. Whether he was lured by the promises of outrageous sex in her letters or whether he naively simply needed a place to stay, no one will ever know. The events of that night have never been fully disclosed.

Three days later, on 2 February 1992, Tracey called her former sweetheart and suggested he call round at her flat in Barking, Essex because she had heard of a property he might want to rent nearby. Tracey was shaking with excitement when she put down the phone. In her twisted, jealous mind it seemed that Jeremy was heading right back into her arms. She decided to prepare herself for his visit in the only way she knew possible …

Knowing she had plenty of time before Jeremy would arrive, Tracey enjoyed a long, soothing bath and thought about what would happen when he turned up. She was determined to lure him with the offer of any kind of sex he wanted. Having had a lustful relationship with him for five months, she believed she knew exactly how to turn him on and there were also a few new tricks she wanted to try out on him.

After her bath, she sprayed herself with her favourite perfume and looked through her wardrobe for her most seductive clothes. She found a tight-fitting black dress that she knew Jeremy liked and then looked through her chest of drawers for a brand-new pair of sheer black nylon panty-hose. Her attention was then caught by the thigh-high black leather boots that she knew were an instant turn-on for most men. The outfit was rounded off by a black suede jacket.

As she rolled on the tights, Tracey could hardly contain her excitement. This was the opportunity she had been waiting for. She was going to exhaust Jeremy with so much sex he would know that she was the woman for him.

Squeezing into the virtually skin-tight leather boots, she smoothed the folds of leather over her knees just as the door bell rang. The sensuous feeling tingling through her body was almost insatiable.

The moment the door opened and Jeremy saw Tracey he knew that he was walking into a sex trap. Despite her excitable state, Tracey realised when she saw the expression on Jeremy's face that seduction would not be an instant event. However, she also had another back-up plan just in case he rejected her. For the first time she was feeling a little nervous and wasn't entirely sure what to do. Then she thought of him with that other woman. That was enough to convince her …

She suddenly whipped out a large kitchen

carving knife. Jeremy was terrified but Tracey was only just beginning. Her voice quivering with jealousy and rage at his immediate rejection, she started to talk about her rival, Linda.

'I went out last night looking for her. I would have used this on her if I'd found her,' she told the shaking Jeremy, who feared that he was about to be killed. He had to think quickly and tried calming her down. He pleaded with Tracey to leave him and Linda alone. He spoke in sensitive detail about their relationship. The glazed mask of determination and hatred on Tracey's face seemed to disappear. She looked in wonderment at her former lover and felt a twinge of sorrow for him.

When she volunteered to make them a cup of coffee, Jeremy sighed with relief. He actually seemed to have avoided a catastrophe.

Over that cup of coffee, Jeremy tried tactfully to let Tracey know that their relationship was well and truly over.

'Please stop pestering us. It's not going to make you any happier and it is not going to change things,' pleaded Jeremy.

Tracey was nodding her head in agreement as her one-time lover spoke. He believed that this might actually mean that his nightmare was over.

'OK. You're right. I will stop,' said Tracey.

Then there was a moment's hesitation in her voice. She would stop, she repeated, but only if Jeremy agreed to sleep with her and allow her to give him oral sex.

Jeremy rocked back and forth on the sofa for a few seconds and said nothing. He could not quite believe that she had just said those words. She interpreted his silence in a completely different way. A seductive smile appeared on the lips of Tracey Gaywood. She got up, walked across the room in those tight black leather boots and mini-dress and tenderly approached him, raising her arm as if to pull him towards her and kiss him. Then she looked at his unresponsive face and immediately knew. With her other hand she slipped something down the side of the sofa.

'No,' uttered Jeremy and pulled away. He felt he could not respond any other way. He did not want her.

At that moment, Jeremy felt what he thought was a punch on the left side of his neck. Then he realised that a sleek boning knife was grasped in Tracey's hand and it was covered in his blood.

Horrifically, the blade had penetrated a vital artery, causing a massive loss of blood. Bright red blood was spurting out of the side of his neck like a water fountain.

Jeremy struggled to his feet and rushed towards the door but then he found that the door handle on the inside of the living-room door had been taken off. Tracey had deliberately removed it in order to guarantee his seduction or his death.

Scraping desperately at the spindles of the lock inside the door, he turned to see Tracey looking as she used to do after they had made love during their earlier relationship — that same expression of the cat who'd got the cream as she licked her lips with pleasure.

Still trying to poke his finger inside the spindle to release the door, he wondered if she would follow through with another knife plunge. Then he felt the blade lunging at him again and again. He tried to fend her off with one arm as he attempted to open the door with the other. Throughout all of this, blood continued to spurt uncontrollably from his neck wound.

Then, somehow, he managed to turn the lock and get the door open.

In the hallway Jeremy was greeted by a sight that summed up the sick and twisted mind of Tracey Gaywood: she had placed a chest of drawers across the front entrance.

It took all of Jeremy's rapidly diminishing strength to push that heavy piece of furniture aside and then he stumbled out into the street, screaming for help.

'Help me! Somebody help me! Please!'

Passing student Joanne Hill, aged eighteen, helped him to struggle into her home. She and her mother then staunched the flow of blood until an ambulance came to take him to hospital where doctors — who feared they were going to lose him — pulled him back from the brink of death.

As doctors battled to save Jeremy's life, detectives raided Tracey's flat but the besotted woman had vanished and was not seen for another thirteen months, when she gave herself up to an officer in London's Regent Street.

In her bedroom, police found one knife with an eight-inch blade, two with seven-inch blades, one with a four-inch blade and a claw hammer, all of which clearly indicated that there was some level of premeditation on Tracey's part.

At the Old Bailey in February 1994, Tracey Gaywood — a schizophrenic who once believed she was possessed by a demon — admitted wounding Jeremy Parkins with intent to cause grievous bodily harm.

The court heard that Tracey, who came from a loving family, was prescribed slimming pills at the age of fourteen after becoming obsessed about her weight. She became addicted and went on to develop severe psychotic breakdown as well as schizophrenia.

Guy Powell, defending, said, 'She is as much a victim as the man she attacked.'

Before sentencing her, Justice Brian Capstick told Tracey: 'I accept you have a loving and supportive family and that you have fallen victim of mental illness. But you deliberately used a knife intending to cause serious harm. You are fortunate the results were not more serious.'

She was ordered to be detained indefinitely in a secure psychiatric hospital until a panel of doctors is convinced she is cured.

Meanwhile Jeremy Parkins is at a secret address,

still living in fear of being killed. One detective involved in the case said: 'He is terrified that if she is ever freed she will come back to get him.'

5

Murder in a Pick-Up

Lindale, in Texas, is one of those places where nothing ever seems to happen, despite the roar of Highway 69 through its heart. There are few men about on weekday mornings, apart from the occasional old boy in one of the sleazy bars on the edge of town or a gaggle of hearty young networkers playing golf on the local course. Most husbands head off to the nearby big cities for work. For the women there are open days at the school, knitting classes, and lots of good deeds to be done.

Jennifer Loving's life appeared normal enough. Her hard-working husband left for work early and got back after dark most nights. They were comfortable financially, but she did find she frequently had a little too much spare time.

Television programmes like *Married with Children* were watched avidly by Jennifer Loving, especially on those long, lonely evenings when her husband Greg decided to down endless beers in one of the local hostelries. Jennifer read little — magazines like the *National Enquirer* were her staple diet. Her chief occupation was bringing up their four-year- old son and going into town to do the shopping. She often spun those trips out most of the day. But there was another aspect to Jennifer's life that she never revealed to anyone: her husband's appalling temper tantrums. Well, that was what they were to start with, but soon they developed into something far worse ...

'Get a fucking move on, woman!'

Greg Loving was waiting outside the bathroom as his wife sat on the toilet. At times, it seemed as if there was no escape, no sanctuary from him.

'I said. Get outta there.'

Suddenly the door burst open and Greg snatched the ragged remains of the toilet roll on the sink next to Jennifer.

'I told you not to use so much goddamn paper, woman!'

Jennifer looked up at him in terror. She had seen that look in his eyes before. They were deep and dark and distant and she knew that meant he was about to beat her. She was trembling. He jerked her off the toilet, bent her over his knee and spanked her naked bottom so hard she could feel the stinging all the way down to her ankles.

'I told you not to use so much goddamn paper woman. I told you!'

He beat her for ten minutes. His breathing became irregular. She sensed he wasn't just using his anger to punish her. She suspected he was getting his kicks from humiliating her. She did not dare struggle because then he would hit her even harder. Finally, he pushed her from his lap and shoved her to the floor. Her bottom was covered in bruises. She began to wonder where it would all end.

It wasn't the first time she had been beaten by Greg and she was certain it would not be the last. Sometimes he would smash her around the living room with his fists, then force her into the bedroom where he would rape her all night long.

When Jennifer told some of her friends in town they said he could not have raped her because he was her husband. Jennifer assured them he did. But the women of Lindale did not really want to know.

This quiet, sleepy town with its population of just 2,500, was renowned as a place where nothing much happened and that was the way everyone in Lindale wanted to keep it. Even when the beatings and sexual attacks grew worse, Jennifer accepted them as part of married life. In any case there were other occasions when Gary could be so pleasant and loving. Sometimes, he would take Jennifer and their son out for picnics in the country. On other occasions, he would shower them with gifts. It was often hard for Jennifer to work out where the good Gary ended and the bad Gary began. She had thought it was connected to alcohol at first, but he eventually began to attack her even when he was stone cold sober.

Other times, Gary himself would recognise he was about to go crazy and he would charge into the back yard or jump in his pick-up to get away, so he could cool off without taking it out on his frail young wife. But one day, in early August 1992, Gary came home from work in a filthy mood. He was ranting and raving about everything from the cost of the shopping to Jennifer's excessive use of washing powder. She tried to walk away from him, but he grabbed her wrist and pulled her down onto his lap. She presumed another beating was about to happen.

But Gary's lip curled up as he looked into her eyes. She tried to look away but she could feel his glare boring into her. Those eyes were nasty, deep and emotionless. They were scaring her. He sat there holding her down on his lap like that for at least five minutes, just silently trying to out-stare his petrified wife. Every time she tried to look away he squeezed her wrist tightly then pulled her round again.

Suddenly he pulled a gun out of his pocket and shoved it to her temple.

This is it, thought Jennifer. *He is going to kill me. It's been on the cards for long enough. Now the time has come. Oh, God make it quick. Please make it quick.*

Jennifer closed her eyes and waited for it to happen. But only silence followed. Then she felt the cold metal of the gun's snub pushing at her mouth.

'Open up, bitch.'

Jennifer was so scared she did nothing at first.

'Open up, BITCH!'

She parted her mouth and felt the cold steel slide between her lips. After pushing three inches of the barrel in, he began easing it backwards and forwards. In and out. She kept her eyes closed throughout. Jennifer could hear her husband's breathing quickening. She dared not think about the perverted images that must have been going through his mind at that moment.

'You want it, don't you, bitch?'

Then, just as suddenly, he shoved much more of the barrel into her mouth and stopped. It was choking her. She presumed he was about to pull the trigger.

CLICK. He pulled.

This is it, she thought. But nothing happened. He was laughing.

'Say bye-bye.'

CLICK. He pulled the trigger.

Nothing happened. He was laughing uncontrollably now. With a quick jerk, he pulled the barrel out from between her lips, scraping her teeth in the process.

'Open your eyes. You're still alive.'

A few days later, Jennifer discovered that she was pregnant. To most married couples this would have been great news, but to Jennifer it represented danger because she was going to have to tell Greg and there was no knowing exactly how he would respond. Just before he came home she managed to find the same gun with which Greg had simulated death and oral sex on her, and made sure it was loaded. This time he was not going to hurt her.

'Shit. That's bad news,' were the first words Greg spoke after Jennifer told him the news of her pregnancy as they sat in the back yard.

'Whose is it, anyhow?'

Jennifer was too frightened to answer.

'I think I'll take the kid and get outta here, now! You whore.'

The words wounded Jennifer. There was no way she would allow him to take their son, and how dare he suggest she was having sex with anyone other than him. He had made these sorts of threats before, but this time he wasn't going to get away with it.

Then she saw that look in his eyes once more and knew trouble was on the horizon. She could feel her hands shaking. She didn't know what to do. Then Greg Loving signed his own death sentence. He began running towards her. She hesitated, but saw those eyes snapping at her and instantly knew she had to do it. Jennifer raised the semi-automatic pistol, aimed right at her husband and squeezed the trigger. This time the gun was loaded. The bullet pierced his head and he crumpled to the ground.

Minutes later, Jennifer somehow managed to hoist her bleeding husband on to the flatbed of his precious pick-up truck. Every now and again he mumbled a few words incoherently.

That's a relief, thought Jennifer. *I want him to stay alive a bit longer. I want him to really suffer.*

Jennifer rushed into the house, grabbed her four-year-old son and placed him in the front seat next to her. She decided to drive 50 miles to her relatives in the city of Longview. That would mean her husband had a slow and painful death as she drove along the bumpy highway. In fact, every time she hit a pothole she smiled to herself because she knew that would increase his pain.

Police officer Sherryl Bolton chose to make law enforcement his career in 1989. He settled in Lindale because he wanted to avoid the big city death and destruction that exists in most of the United States. This was going to be the perfect place to work and raise a family. A private, shy man, Bolton had no desire for glory, just a genuine interest in the good of the common man. He had left his native state of Louisiana and lived for a while in Houston, Texas, a metropolitan area besieged by crime. In Houston, Bolton was shocked by the blatant disregard for the law. It seemed as if no-one cared. The daily onslaught of death and destruc-tion convinced Bolton that he was in need of somewhere more gentle and he figured a small town like Lindale would be the perfect place for him to contribute to keeping the peace.

Lindale's Chief of Police, Mike Rutherford, was a veteran cop who considered Bolton to be a fine officer. His quiet, cautious habits were well appreciated in the town where rip-roaring cowboy behaviour was definitely not appreciated. Rutherford knew that Sherryl Bolton was more than capable of handling a big case if required.

Life in Lindale seemed as peaceful as ever on the hot, sticky night of August 10 1992. The trees in the pine woods surrounding the town were creaking in the scorching heat. In the distance there was an occasional rumble from one of the big 18-wheel tractor-trailer rigs negotiating the red lights as they rushed through town on Highway 69. Frequently, the backfires and blowouts from the i8-wheelers could sound like gunshots. So, when a loud pop rang through the air at 9:30pm that night, no one gave it a second thought.

Fifty miles away, in Longview, Texas (population 50,000), law officers were dealing with the sort of crimes that Sherryl Bolton hated. Dispatchers and cops were breaking up domestic incidents, shutting down rowdy bars, plucking accident victims off the streets and dealing with a string of burglaries. When the Longview Police Department was called out to a shooting on the edge of the city, it was nothing unusual. There were about a dozen such incidents every month in the city. Dead at the scene was Greg Loving, a 39-year-old self employed construction worker, the son of the former postmaster of the smaller town of Lindale. Loving's brother-in-law had called police to tell them about a body which had showed up at his residence. He had not even realised at first glance that it was a relative.

Longview investigators found Loving's corpse sprawled in the back of his pick-up truck parked out front of the house. Pools of blood filled the bed of the truck. Also at the scene was Greg Loving's wife Jennifer. She calmly explained to police that her husband had been despondent and had shot himself, following a family argument. She told the officers all this in a manner that suggested complete control of the situation. There were no tears, there was little emotion, just a very matter-of-fact style delivery. It was almost as if she was talking about someone who was not even related to her. In fact, she was describing the scene as if she was a cop.

Longview police lieutenant Mike Satterwhite was puzzled by the apparent coolness of the victim's wife. It bothered him a great deal, but for the moment he had nothing more than a hunch to go on. In his mind he couldn't say for certain whether it was murder or suicide. He was also deeply bothered by the fact that it appeared that Greg Loving had been shot several hours earlier. Why hadn't the police been called sooner? And why didn't they take Loving to the hospital? After taking a statement from 25-year-old Jennifer Loving, police in Lindale were notified of the killing because that was where the Lovings lived. Lt Satterwhite advised Lindale that they should handle the investigation because he firmly believed the shooting had taken place at the Lovings' home the previous evening. In Lindale, Chief Rutherford was puzzled by the request to take over the investigation, but decided that he should put Sherryl Bolton on the case anyhow. For Bolton — woken in the middle of the night and told he was chief investigator on a homicide inquiry — it was a baptism of fire. He had never been involved in a murder investigation and, to make matters worse, this one had actually ended in a city fifty miles away.

But within hours, Bolton and crime scene investigator Jason Waller were reviewing all the information they had on the case. They rapidly concluded that they should ask for a warrant to search the Lovings' neat, detached house in the older section on the east side of town. Jennifer Loving did not bat an eyelid when Bolton and his team knocked on her front door and demanded entry to the house. The officers combed the area very carefully and soon uncovered several weapons, including a .22 calibre semi-automatic pistol hidden under a mattress in the couple's bedroom. They immediately brought Mrs Loving in for questioning.

At first, the grieving wife retold the same suicide story she had given the Longview police the previous night.

'We were drinking beer about 10 o'clock in the evening and I told Greg I was pregnant again,' she explained quietly and calmly. 'He got angry and went into the back yard to be alone.'

Greg, she explained to the officers, always liked to be alone when he was upset. Jennifer insisted that Greg had been completely thrown by the news of impending fatherhood because he wasn't ready to have another child 'just now'. Jennifer then lowered her voice to a virtual whisper as she told officers that she stayed inside the house for half an hour more with their four-year-old son while Greg continued sulking outside. Later, she became curious when Greg did not come back inside the house. She claimed that, when she finally decided to look for him, she found him slumped unconscious over the tailgate of their pick-up truck. Greg had shot himself. She said she had heard a pop earlier, but ignored it because she thought it was a firecracker or one of those trucks thundering through town.

'I found him in the back of the pick-up and he looked like he was dead. I checked him for a pulse and I could not find one. I figured he had shot himself in the head because he had blood on his face and I found a gun laying on the ground.'

Then Jennifer switched the subject around to herself. It startled the investigators. 'I didn't shoot my husband and I don't think anyone else did.'

Officer Bolton was intrigued by this response because it certainly seemed to suggest that Jennifer had a guilty conscience, if nothing else. She then told in vivid detail how she pushed his body onto the rough metal flatbed of the truck and began to drive towards Longview, where her closest relatives lived. She believed that her brother would know what to do and would calm her down. She did not have any place else to turn.

But, as the questioning continued, more and more inconsistencies emerged in her story.

Investigators were soon in absolutely no doubt that she was covering up the truth. Jennifer became more and more nervous. Suddenly, she cracked and broke down and cried. She admitted pulling the trigger of the gun but insisted it had gone off unexpectedly in her hands. The young wife then said she had become upset when she thought Greg was going to move away and take their son with him. She admitted being a little drunk, but continued to insist that the shooting was an accident.

But, when investigators questioned other family and friends, they dismissed her claims yet again, especially since police had been called to the residence to break up numerous domestic disputes. Jennifer also had her fair share of drinking trophies. These included a conviction for driving while intoxicated in neighbouring Wood County. She was still serving felony probation for that offence at the time of her husband's shooting.

Eventually, the investigators uncovered enough evidence to bring the case before a Grand Jury. Officer Bolton and Sgt David Craft of the Lindale Police Department obtained a warrant for her arrest. A bond was set at $40,000.

In November 1993, the murder trial of Jennifer Loving was held in the 7th District Court of Judge Louis Gohmert, a young attorney who had just been elected to the bench. The trial was heard in the Smith County Courthouse in Tyler, about 15 miles north of Lindale. By the time proceedings had begun Jennifer had changed her story again. She now admitted the shooting had not been an accident, but she pleaded self-defence to the murder charge, on the basis that her husband had been violent to her when she told him she thought she might be pregnant.

One of the prime defence witnesses was Dr Robert Geffner of the Family Violence and Sexual Assault Institute. Dr Geffner testified that he believed Jennifer had Battered Woman's Syndrome and that her mental problems and severe stress had been caused by the abuse that led to the shooting. The doctor described the condition as causing a 'numbing where they (the women) psychologically numb themselves not to feel'. Dr Geffner added, 'When the syndrome strikes the woman blacks out her thoughts in a psychological amnesia where it's so painful the brain tries to keep certain thoughts out of the mind.'

Dr Geffner, who is also a psychology professor at the University of Texas at Tyler, said Jennifer appeared to have been physically, mentally and sexually abused. His official diagnosis had been developed over a nine-month period and included some 15 separate tests. He also indicated she was suffering from 'post traumatic stress disorder' as a result of the shooting. The doctor insisted that Jennifer was in a confused mental state that night and 'it took her a long time to realize what shape the victim was in.'

In her statement to Lindale Police, Jennifer had said, 'I kept expecting him to get up and beat me.'

The defence team noted that the post traumatic stress disorder would explain her peculiar actions that night when she left Greg in the truck. Jennifer's defence attorney also gave the court examples of appalling episodes described to him by Jennifer. Several of the incidents involved her claims of forced sex and beatings.

The physician noted that, despite what happened, 'to this day it appears she still loves him and wishes the shooting hadn't happened. She wanted them to remain as a family. She just didn't want to be hit any more.' Prosecutors insisted that Jennifer Loving was more than capable of looking after herself and they brought in several witnesses who testified to her own violent behaviour. One neighbour had the court in laughter when she said, 'If Jennifer went into the woods hunting bear with a toothpick, she'd come out the winner.'

Prosecutors argued that Jennifer carefully set up the murder and intended to carry Greg's body to Longview to dispose of it, until relatives intervened and called in the police. They also insisted that Jennifer should have sought a divorce from her husband if she had been as badly beaten as she claimed.

The jury deliberated for five hours, before returning a guilty verdict. The ten women and two men on the jury did not believe that her response to her brutal husband had been justifiable. After another four hours of deliberation, jurors assessed Jennifer's punishment at 92 years in prison. They chose the number 92 to remind Jennifer of the year she murdered her husband.

FOOTNOTE: *This remarkable case took one more turn before it could he closed. Jennifer was placed in the Smith County Jail, in Tyler, to await her transfer to the state prison. When she and several other female inmates returned from the exercise yard, Jennifer saw an opportunity to escape. She slipped her small wrists out of her handcuffs and broke into a run. The startled guard escorting the inmates decided to stay with the other prisoners rather than give chase. Loving rapidly discarded her orange jail uniform and bolted through the front door of the courthouse, which is equipped with bars and locked only from the outside, in compliance with fire regulations. Police were soon in hot pursuit as the other inmates cheered Jennifer on, who soon became lost in the crowds on the streets of downtown Tyler.*

The Sherrif's department in Lindale was immediately notified of the escape and police surveillance was put on the Lovings' house. Officer Bolton was deeply disappointed that Jennifer had escaped. But Jennifer Loving wanted no part of Lindale after all the beatings and abuse she had suffered at the hands of her husband in that small town. She headed in the opposite direction. Jennifer had sneaked to a downtown Tyler church, wearing only white boxer shorts and a T-shirt. There she had made several phone calls and found extra clothing.

Then she and a boyfriend headed to a motel 15 miles outside Tyler. Acting on an anonymous tip, officers tracked down Loving and arrested her — it was just five hours after her escape.

Jennifer's only comment when caught was, 'Okay, you got me.' She smiled broadly at photographers and news reporters as officers placed her in handcuffs and led her back to jail. District Attorney Skeen filed charges of felony escape, a third-degree felony punishable by two to ten years in prison and a fine of up to $5,000 upon conviction. Meanwhile, Sheryl Bolton earned his own reward for bringing Jennifer to justice. The young officer was chosen by the Lindale City Council to be the new Chief of Police in the town.

In the eyes of many women, Jennifer Loving is not a criminal, but a heroine who took the law into her own hands ...

6

For Whom the Bell Tolls

The shrill sound of a bell ringing loudly in the distance meant only one thing to Judy Benkowski — her husband was demanding something.

Clarence Benkowski was overweight and overbearing. All his life he had been number one in that miserable household. Even now, after retiring from his job as a welder, he expected to be waited upon hand and foot.

When his sick and aged mother decided to move in, things became even worse for Judy because it meant that now there were two of them bullying and cursing her: making her wait on them like a serf, treating her like dirt. There had to be a better life somewhere else, surely?

Often the two obese specimens would sit in the armchairs in the sitting room of their neat, detached suburban home at Number 508, South Yale Avenue, Addison, near Chicago, for hours on end without budging. That was when the little bell rang the most. An endless stream of demands followed.

Ring: 'Get me a coffee,' said one.

Ring: 'Get me a beer,' said the other.

Ring: 'This coffee's cold, get me another.'

Ring: 'This beer's not cold enough. Why haven't you kept them in the freezer?'

So it went on and on and on. Judy had no time for a job and only a small handful of friends in the entire world.

Her only occupation was looking after those two leeches, as well as bringing up her two sons.

Not surprisingly, it often got too much for her. Her life was so relentless and so unenjoyable. She would cry herself to sleep at night, wondering when it would ever end. Occasionally, Clarence would drunkenly try to have sex with her. It certainly wasn't making love. in fact, it seemed more closely aligned to rape than anything else.

The act of sex was totally one-sided. He would make her fondle him and then — the moment he was ready — she would just lie there and listen to him grunting. Often she would try to think of other things, like the next day's shopping. Then he would hurt her with his roughness and that would snap her back to the unpleasant reality of having a huge fat lump of lard molesting her. The only good thing was that it was usually over in minutes, if not seconds. But there was so much pain involved. It was the sort of pain that inevitably occurs when an overweight old man forces himself on a slightly-built, five-foot-tall woman more than twenty years his junior. They might have been husband and wife in law but they were total strangers in every other sense of the word.

One day, however, Clarence decided he wanted to spice up his sex life, so he bought a waterbed. Typically, it was the cheapest one he could find and had the unpleasant side effect of being so overfilled that it made its occupants feel seasick.

The result was that Judy still lay there as usual every time he wanted sex — only now she had the horrible, overwhelming sensation of rocking up and down as if on a boat bobbing across the ocean.

It did help in one respect, however. Judy usually felt so nauseous within seconds of Clarence starting that he would often stop rather than risk being puked over.

Basically, Clarence's attitude towards sex was much the same as his outlook on life: men ruled the household, women were just there to honour and obey. He wasn't interested in Judy's feelings, he just wanted four big square meals a day and sex on demand.

For almost twenty years, Judy had put up with the insults and the appalling stress of married life. What else could she do? She had no career, no existence outside those four walls. She had been trapped for so long that she had forgotten what it was like to enjoy herself.

'You cannot let him treat you like this. You've got to do something about it, Judy.'

Debra Santana was outraged by her friend's complete acceptance of her distressing marital situation. She had heard so many horror stories from Judy. How could a husband treat his wife so badly? Debra assured her friend that she certainly would not put up with it.

Judy protested in her quiet, reserved way, 'What can I do? I have nowhere to go. No means of support.'

However, Debra was determined to help her friend and neighbour. Theirs was an unlikely friendship. Debra was a striking blonde aged thirty-two with a fun-loving attitude towards life, who had suffered during her marriage and taken the easy way out — divorce. She was enjoying everything that Judy had long since given up hope of ever seeing.

The main object of envy between the two women was Debra's athletic, black lover who gave her all-round satisfaction and never treated her badly. Judy was very jealous of Debra's lifestyle. She so wanted to feel warmth, passion and true love again. Judy knew Debra was right when she said she had to do something. But what?

Clarence, a strict Catholic, would not even discuss the subject of divorce. It wouldn't have been so bad if he had been prepared to let them lead separate lives. Then she could have gone out with other men and he could have done as he pleased. However, Clarence believed he owned Judy lock, stock and barrel. She was his woman. If he wanted instant sex, he should get it. If he wanted to insult her, he could. If he wanted her to be his slave, nothing could stop him, or so he told Judy with great relish.

Debra told Judy that there was no way she should accept this for the rest of her life. She might be thirteen years younger than Judy but Judy was finding herself increasingly influenced by her younger, more outrageous neighbour. The more they talked about Debra's adventures, the more Judy began to realise how desperate she was to end the misery.

'But what can I do about him?' Judy asked her friend one day.

'I've got an idea …' replied Debra.

Eddie Brown had given Debra all the sexual satisfaction she had ever craved. Even fully clothed, his muscular torso was literally bursting his shirt buttons. Judy Benkowski felt a tingle of excitement as she shook his hand for the first time. She imagined that Debra must have enjoyed some outrageous sex with this handsome stud. Only one thing about Eddie did surprise Judy: he was just five foot three inches tall. In fact, Debra towered over him by a good four inches.

'Not only is Eddie great in bed, but he's also going to help you with your problem, Judy,' chipped in Debra when all three met up.

Debra, Judy and Eddie had business to discuss

because Debra had convinced Judy that Eddie was going to be the perfect man for a very special job for Judy. And it was a job that required a certain amount of planning.

'Do you really think you can kill him without being caught?' Judy had to confront him with the facts about the job at hand. He had told Debra he could murder Judy's husband with 'no trouble'. He had even agreed a fee of $5,000. However, they had to sort out details like where it should be done, what weapon should be used, how they could make sure the police did not suspect anything. What if he lived?

For a few moments, Judy wondered if she had gone completely crazy. How could she even contemplate murdering another human being? It all seemed like a dream. She hesitated. 'Maybe we should rethink all this.'

There was brief silence from her two accomplices.

'What?' said Debra. 'You can't change your mind. We agreed on this, Judy. Come on. Let's do it!'

Then Eddie chipped in, 'Yeah. It'll be easy. We can make it look like a burglary. No problem.'

The pressure was mounting on Judy. She wasn't a strong-willed woman at the best of times. She felt as if there was no choice in the matter. This was her only possible escape route from a miserable life. This was the one answer to all her problems and unhappiness. Certainly it seemed drastic, but then what more did that animal of a husband deserve? He had treated her like dirt for too long. Now it was her turn. Revenge would seem sweet. There was no turning back.

First there was the small matter of how and where to do it.

It was mid-October 1988, and Hallowe'en was fast approaching. Judy had a great idea, she told her two partners in crime. 'Eddie, I'll get you a real scary costume. You're so short you'll look just like a kid out trick or treating. Then you'll knock on the door, Clarence will answer and you'll blast him away with a gun after saying "trick or treat".'

Debra and Eddie looked stunned. It was a preposterous plan and they knew it but Judy seemed really attracted to the ghoulish aspects of it. She even laughed excitedly as she described the plot. 'He never likes to give anything to anyone who comes knocking at the door. I kinda like the idea of him getting the ultimate "trick".'

The earlier, hesitant Judy had been completely replaced by a hard-nosed would-be killer getting into the mood to murder. Her hunger for his death surprised even her two friends. She had now fully accepted the whole plan as fait accompli. The risks involved were being outweighed by the fast approaching scenario — a new life without Clarence. Judy was feeling happier than she had done for years.

'But hang on there, Judy,' said Eddie. 'Trick or treaters don't tend to gun down their customers. The cops would know it was a contract hit straight off and they'd get us for sure.'

Eddie was trying desperately to defuse the

situation. He had agreed to murder this woman's husband because the guy sounded like he deserved it, but the scheme Judy had just described was absolutely insane. It was like something out of a comic book, hardly the sort of low-key killing Eddie had in mind.

Judy was having none of it. She reckoned it was the perfect plan. 'The cops will think some crazy trick or treater is out there blasting innocent people to death. They'll never suss it as a contract killing.'

Debra and Eddie glanced at each other and shrugged their shoulders.

'You're the boss, lady,' said Eddie. Jobless and just out of jail, he needed the money, so he wasn't about to blow the contract, whatever the risks.

Hallowe'en trick or treating involves children dressed in spooky ghost or witch costumes knocking on the doors of houses in their street and shouting 'trick or treat' when someone comes to the door. Inevitably, a liberal helping of sweets is offered to the children and everyone goes home happy.

In the Chicago suburb of Addison, they tended to celebrate Hallowe'en just as fervently as in the rest of the United States, where the tradition first emerged thanks to the activities of a group of devil worshippers more than two hundred years ago.

South Yale Avenue — where the Benkowskis lived — was as traditional as it was typical: row upon row of three-bedroomed detached bungalows built to maximise the use of the space available. It was classic middle-American suburbia.

On the night of Hallowe'en that year, Eddie Brown began to wonder what he had got himself into. As Judy and Debra adjusted the ghoulish face mask they had bought for him at the local store, he felt that dressing up like a kid going out trick or treating contrasted rather disturbingly with his real mission as a professional killer seeking to murder a housewife's elderly husband.

To make matters worse, the latex mask was very uncomfortable. The two women had insisted on getting one that covered his entire face so that no one could see what colour his skin was. However, it was so airless behind that mask that Eddie was thinking he might never make it to number 508 alive! He was gasping for air before he'd even left the house.

'This is crazy. I can't even see properly out of the eye slits.'

Eddie's voice was so badly muffled by the mask that the two women did not even hear him at first.

So he yelled: 'I SAID THIS IS CRAZY.'

If Eddie was going to have to shout this loudly to be heard, then he'd probably alert the entire street when he went knocking on Clarence's door to announce his trick or treating campaign.

Eddie was about to walk out into the street when his face dropped. (Well, it would have if he had not had that latex mask on.) There were dozens of children wandering up and down the street in their trick or treating disguises. It was almost as if the entire population of under-fifteen-year-olds in

Addison had decided to hit South Yale at exactly the same time.

Eddie ripped off the mask in a fit of fury and started to jump up and down on the spot in his white skeleton costume. The two women looked at him incredulously.

'I am not doing this. I can't start shooting at the guy in front of all those kids. I'll never get away with it.'

The entire plan had always had a ring of insanity about it. He decided to abandon it there and then before it was too late.

Judy was furious. She had hoped that she was just twenty-four hours away from never having to see that ugly hulk of a husband again. Now Eddie had ruined all her hopes and desires. 'But we have to do it, Eddie. You cut a deal.'

Judy was getting very angry but Eddie had no intention of not carrying out the killing. He just felt it needed a new plan. 'Don't get me wrong, Judy. I will kill him. But not tonight. It would be crazy and we'd all end up in jail.'

Judy reluctantly agreed with him. 'OK, but we gotta do it soon.'

Ring: 'Where's my breakfast?'

Ring: 'Come on, I'm hungry.'

Ring ... ring ... ring ...

Clarence Benkowski was giving his usual pre-breakfast performance in precisely the same way he had done for the previous twenty years. His mother was visiting relatives so at least Judy didn't have to tolerate her. In the kitchen, Judy muttered quietly under her breath: 'Don't worry. You'll get just what you deserve in good time.'

If Clarence had not been so incredibly lazy, he might have got up from the breakfast table where he was slouched and lumbered into the kitchen to witness Judy pouring the contents of twenty sachets of sleeping pills into his coffee. Instead, he just kept on ringing. Ring: 'Move your ass woman. I'm hungry.'

Clarence was actually helping to sentence himself to death. Ringing that bloody bell yet again was the signal that marked the beginning of the end of his life, for it guaranteed that Judy felt no guilt as she emptied the contents of those packets and then swilled them around in his coffee. The more he rang the bell, the better she felt about killing him. It was a wonderful feeling just to contemplate the end of such an awful era in her life.

'Just keep ringing, Clarence. Just keep ringing. Soon you will never get another chance.'

Judy's only error was rather stupidly to tip the empty pill packets into the trash can before moving towards the dining area with a spring in her step, a bounce in her walk.

'There you go, sweetheart.'

She hadn't called him that for years. 'Sweetheart' was a term of endearment. How could she even contemplate feeling warmth towards the man she was about to have murdered? But Judy's passions were already rising at the very thought of his demise. She felt a tingle of excitement as she put the tray down on the breakfast table.

She sat at the table and sipped quietly at her tea but her eyes kept straining upwards and across the table towards Clarence. He hadn't got anywhere near that coffee yet.

Clarence was a predictable creature of habit. He liked to gulp down his fried eggs first and then stuff some toast in that big fat mouth of his. Judy knew that cup of coffee would soon be lifted to his lips. *'Be patient. Relax. He's going to drink it. All in good time. All in good time.'*

The Chicago-Sun Times was spread across the table in front of Clarence, as it always was each morning. Something caught his eye. He stopped eating and gasped at the sports results.

Not once had he ever made conversation with Judy over breakfast, or any other time for that matter. Clarence was not about to break the habit of a lifetime, but the cup of coffee remained untouched. Judy's initial burst of excitement was rapidly turning to desperation. *'Come on! Come on! Get on with it!'*

She was feeling desperate. It was time for desperate measures. 'Sweetheart,' for some weird reason she used that word again. 'Sweetheart, drink your coffee or it'll get cold.'

For a split second, Clarence looked at his wife quizzically. She *never* spoke at breakfast. Why the hell was she nagging him to drink his coffee? Never before in more than twenty years. Why now?

However, as with most things in Clarence's life,

he gave it only a brief thought. Any further analysis would have been completely out of character.

Judy was annoyed with herself for weakening in the face of such adversity. What on earth was she doing trying to make him drink the coffee? It was a sure way to guarantee he'd get suspicious. She did not dare to look up again in case he caught her eye and saw the signs of guilt. He might even read the murderous intentions that filled her mind every moment as they sat at that fateful last breakfast.

Judy was getting very anxious. Maybe she had blown it? Perhaps he'd sussed her out? She shut her eyes for a split second in the hope that all that doubt and anguish would go away. Then it happened. The harsh slurping noise was like music to her ears. She opened her eyes once more to see that he was gulping it down at a furious rate, desperately trying to wash all that food down his big, ugly gullet. Now he was about to pay the ultimate price for his greed.

First one whole cup went down, then another in quick succession. Judy could feel the rush of relief running through her veins. She sighed quietly to herself It was one of the most satisfying moments of her life.

'I don't feel so good. I think I'll lie down a while.'

The sleeping pills were at last taking effect. Eddie had provided very precise instructions on how many she should feed him. Just enough to knock him into a deep slumber rather than complete unconsciousness. That way no one would be able to tell he had been drugged.

Just then Clarence got up and struggled towards the bedroom. He only just managed to reach that wretched waterbed before collapsing in a heap. Judy crept into the room after him, just to make sure he was out. Then she phoned Debra and told her, 'He's asleep. You better tell Eddie and get over here.'

Judy slarnmed down the phone and awaited her two accomplices.

Debra was the first to arrive at the house. She hugged Judy warmly in an effort to show her good friend that she supported her completely and utterly. The two women sat side by side on the sofa in the front room and counted the minutes until Eddie arrived. They soon heard the back door opening and then their hired killer walked in.

In an eerie silence, Judy handed Eddie her husband's World War Two Luger pistol and motioned him towards the master bedroom. They did not want to risk waking Clarence. Meanwhile, Debra put on a pair of stereo headphones and started listening to heavy rock music. It was a bizarre reaction. Maybe she was trying to blot out the noise of the gunfire that was about to occur?

The two women sat together on the sofa. Eddie had earlier said he would use a pillow to muffle the sound of the gun but Judy still heard the muffled pops of the three bullets being fired into her husband. It was nothing like what she had expected, but she showed no emotion. At last it was over.

However, there was still work to be done. Judy and her two friends had to make it look like a burglary that had gone wrong. The two women and Brown began tearing the house apart in convincing fashion. They pulled drawers of clothes out and spread them all over the bed where Clarence lay. Incredibly, the waterbed was still intact, despite the rain of bullets. Judy was disappointed in a way because she really did hate that waterbed. On the other hand it would have caused such a mess if it had leaked everywhere.

Meanwhile, Eddie was smashing the place to bits to make it look like a genuine burglary. Some of his blatant destruction was proving much more stressful to Judy than the murder of her husband.

'No. Not the china, please.'

Judy would not allow Eddie to destroy her vast collection of china. She had lovingly collected it over many years and it was the one of the few things in that house that she cared about. Eddie was incensed. 'But this is supposed to look like a burglary!'

'Just leave it. We can still make it look good without wrecking my china.'

Eddie just shrugged his shoulders. She was paying him so it was up to her.

A few minutes later, it was time for Eddie to make his escape out of the back door. First there was the matter of payment. Judy handed over one thousand dollars as his first instalment and also allowed Eddie to take two rings from a jewellery drawer. The rest of the cash would be given to him within a week. Seconds later Eddie was gone.

Debra could clearly see the relief on Judy's face.

The two women embraced. They had done it. They had got rid of the animal. There was a big wide world out there waiting to be conquered. Judy was about to start her new life. However, before they could leave the ransacked house, they needed to make sure the coast was clear. First, Judy checked down the street. It was mid-morning. Husbands were at work; mothers were out shopping. Not a person in sight.

The Italian restaurant where Judy and Debra went to celebrate was so crowded that they were hardly noticed. The only unusual thing about them was that they ordered a bottle of very expensive white wine. As few people drink alcohol at lunchtime in middle America, their toast to one another did not go completely unnoticed.

'To us. Long may we live without husbands.' The two women chuckled like naughty schoolgirls.

It wasn't just a new life of freedom that Judy was looking forward to; she believed Clarence's life insurance would be worth at least $100,000 and then there was the one $150,000 mortgage-paid house. Judy Benkowski was going to be a very merry widow indeed.

'He's been murdered. He's been murdered.'

Judy's screeching tones sounded truly horrific to Addison cop, Detective Sergeant Tom Gorniak. He had been patched through to the Benkowski home after the nearby police station had received an emergency call from Debra and Judy, who had 'discovered' Clarence shot dead on their return from a 'shopping trip'.

In a bizarre, three-way conference call involving his patrol car, the police-station switchboard and Judy, Gorniak was trying to ascertain what had happened as he drove at high speed to South Yale Avenue.

By the time he rolled up at the house, an ambulance had already arrived. Gorniak immediately consoled the two women and got a uniformed officer to escort them from the property.

Then he began a detailed inspection of the premises. He knew he could not disturb anything until the crime-scene technicians arrived, but he was well aware that this was the best time to look around because everything was untouched and exactly as it had been at the time of the murder. He rapidly became puzzled by certain aspects of the crime.

The victim's body lay slumped in bed as if he had been taking an afternoon nap. How could he have slept through the noise of an intruder who then leant over him and fired three bullets into his head at close range?

Gorniak knew that few burglars would do that. In fact, even in trigger-happy America few burglars carry guns. A good burglar just gets the hell out of a house the moment he is disturbed. If someone stumbles upon him, his first response is to run, not shoot.

No, thought Gorniak, this victim was asleep

when he was shot. He did not even have time to turn around and see who his killer was.

Then the policeman noticed the clothes thrown from the drawers over the body. That meant the killer had ransacked the room after the shooting. It just did not make sense. The intruder would have got out of there as fast as possible following the shooting.

Gorniak had been a policeman for ten years. He knew how dangerous it was to draw any conclusions at such an early stage in a murder inquiry, but he had no doubt that this looked like a contract killing.

'Did your husband have any enemies, Mrs Benkowski?'

Det. Sgt. Gorniak was trying to be as gentle as possible. After all, this was the apparently grieving widow he was talking to, and she appeared to be really badly cut up.

'No,' Judy replied. 'He had no enemies.'

Gorniak had a hunch. It was nothing more than that but it was enough to make him persuade Judy to stay on at the police station for a little longer that evening. He explained to her that he knew how awful she must be feeling but it really would be in everyone's interests if she stayed behind. Judy agreed. She did not want to appear to be hindering the police inquiries in any way.

Gorniak and his colleague Detective Mike Tierney began gently probing the widow for clues. They were convinced that there was still a lot more to tell about this case.

Judy, meanwhile, was getting edgy. She knew she had to tell them something. Maybe a half truth would solve her problems. Then they would leave her alone, surely? 'I did see someone outside the house this morning,' she recalled anxiously to the two detectives.

Gorniak and Tierney raised their eyebrows. Why didn't she mention this before? Judy then described in vivid detail how she had returned from her shopping trip with her friend and they had seen this rather short, stocky black man.

'He seemed to be running away from the house,' explained Judy.

The two officers were very surprised. They started to pull in the reins a little bit. They sensed that Judy knew more than she was revealing.

The next step was to haul Judy's friend Debra Santana in for questioning. As the detectives waited with Judy for her friend to arrive, they tried an old and trusted technique.

'It would help us if you could tell us everything you know,' said Gorniak.

Judy waited for a moment. She had a lot on her mind and those officers were well aware of it. 'I think I knew the black guy who was running from my house. His name is Eddie Brown. He is Debra's boyfriend.'

Tom Gorniak and Mike Tierney raised their eyebrows. They knew they were about to hear a full confession to murder.

In September 1989, Judy Benkowski cried when she was sentenced to one hundred years in prison for hiring hit-man Eddie Brown to murder her husband.

Du Page County prosecutor Michael Fleming had argued that Benkowski should receive the death penalty but Judge Brian Telander ruled that there were mitigating factors that 'precluded the imposition of the death penalty'. These included no prior criminal record, numerous health problems and several character witnesses who testified on her behalf.

Fleming described the sentence — which means that Benkowski will not be eligible for parole until she is ninety-seven as 'fair and appropriate. She claimed she wanted a divorce and he wouldn't go along, but she never even talked to a lawyer about it.'

On 31 August 1991, Benkowski married her sweetheart Clarence Jeske at the Dwight Correctional Institute in Illinois. The couple had first met before her husband was murdered but they both insist their relationship did not begin until after the killing.

By a strange twist of fate, Jeske now lives in that same house where Clarence was murdered in South Yale Avenue. He has even been made legal guardian of Judy's two children by her marriage to Benkowski.

7

Do Unto Others...

They looked every inch the happy couple.

She was blonde, slightly round-faced. With her long hair swept back off her forehead, maybe she more resembled a member of the swinging sixties than the 1990s, but there was a definite attractiveness about her. Despite being just 29 she also had a certain homeliness that comes with being a young mother. It was a pleasant enough combination.

He was tall and dark with a neatly trimmed moustache. Well built. Even slightly cumbersome. He often looked less than his 35 years. And the only real clue to his profession were his hands. He had large, stubby fingers with incredibly short nails — a sure sign of his work as a labourer.

Paul and Pamela Sainsbury hardly warranted a second glance inside the crowded Carinas Nightclub, in the picturesque seaside town of Sidmouth, in Devon. As the soul music throbbed relentlessly from the huge speakers that hung on every wall, the scene resembled a cattle market. For it was the in place for anyone under 40. Groups of men and women would swarm into Carinas on a Saturday night looking for fun and excitement. Many of them were also looking for sex.

Gangs of young men would patrol the disco floor looking for suitable girls to ask for a dance, many of whom had their own secret code that would pronounce their availability. If they were looking to be picked up, they would stay huddled in little groups near the dance floor, sipping slowly on their rum and blackcurrants in the hope that some white knight would ask them for a dance and maybe even offer them a refill.

Other groups of women, intent on just enjoying each other's company, would go straight out onto the dance floor and put their handbags on the floor between them as they danced to the music. It was their special way of saying 'We are not available.' Sometimes they would dance for hours, perfectly happy not to attract the company of any males. Meanwhile, those predatory guys would be filling themselves up with lager — the staple diet of 90% of all men in that club on most nights.

All this meant that by about 11pm, there were always quite a lot of inebriated people in Carinas —

and this particular evening was no exception.

Paul Sainsbury may have had his pretty wife Pam for company but that didn't stop him supping a lot of pints that night. It was his idea of a good night out. In any case, Carinas meant something really special to them — it was the place where they first met eight years earlier. It held a lot of sweet memories for Paul. It reminded him how lucky he was to have Pam. How fortunate he was that she was the mother of his two children.

Yes, Paul really did appear to have a domestic set up that was the envy of many of his friends. And, as he sat with Pam and a few of their local pals at a table near the dance floor, he was no doubt able to reflect on that good fortune. For many of his male friends were still reduced to trying to pick up women in Carinas or any other club for that matter. It was something he did not need to concern himself about. He had Pam. He really loved Pam. She was his life and soul. She was the perfect reflection of his inner self. She understood his weaknesses and nurtured his strengths. They were good together.

Pam, meanwhile, was delighted to be at the nightclub. It was a rare excursion out of the house for her. These days she hardly ever seemed to get out. Maybe, she thought to herself that evening, maybe I should try it more often.

It was difficult to converse above the throbbing beat of the disco, so Pam and Paul found themselves looking around the club, inspecting the vast crowd — many of whom they knew. After all, Sidmouth is one of those sort of places. Most people know each other, even if it is only by sight. And a lot of the men and women gathered at Carinas that night had virtually grown up together. They had gone to the same schools. They had drunk at the same bars and they often went out with the same women (or men).

Pam was slightly different though. She had not grown up in the Victorian town that looked out over one of the prettiest coastlines in Britain. She had been just another holidaymaker when she had visited the town in the early 1980s. But the moment she set eyes on Paul she had known she wanted to be with him — and now Sidmouth was her only home.

But, not being a local had its compensations. It meant that people were more curious about Pam. She had a certain mystique about her and she spoke with a much posher accent than her rough and tumble West Country husband. Many of her neighbours had been really impressed when they heard Pam had been to an expensive private school. In fact she had even been a prefect. But Paul had put all that high-class nonsense firmly behind her. She was his wife now — and he didn't want to even think about the rich and exclusive world she came from.

He didn't like all that sort of talk one bit. Some of his friends reckoned it was because he had a chip on his shoulder about being 'common.' Paul just insisted all that 'rich folk talk' got on his nerves.

Like any reasonably attractive woman, Pam

enjoyed flattery and attention. It was nice to be appreciated. Unfortunately, she rarely had an opportunity to meet that many new friends these days. That made her visit to Carinas all the more enjoyable. She was actually able to come into contact with other people.

She had specially washed and ironed her favourite white dress for that evening. It was not often she had the chance to wear it. As she sipped slowly on her own non-alcoholic drink, she was aware of occasional looks from some of the men who passed by their table. At first, she did not look up as she felt a touch embarrassed. But there seemed to be so many single men out there.

Across the table, Paul was studying the women in much the same way the men were examining his wife. Some of them looked really cracking, he thought to himself. If only I was single again. Paul especially liked the ones in their early twenties who tended to favour short, skin-tight skirts combined with dangerously high stiletto heeled shoes. A new one seemed to drift past his table every other second. Where did all this talent come from?

Ironically, it was only when the numbers of single, pretty girls started to disperse that Paul noticed a man standing nearby leaning against a pillar ever so casually. He seemed to be looking over his way. But then again perhaps he wasn't.

For a few moments, Paul ignored the man. But when he glanced back in his direction he was still there. What was he looking at? Paul turned to face his wife and momentarily caught sight of her eyes. They were definitely pointed in the direction of that man. What the hell was happening?

Pam had only given the man the briefest of glances after she had felt his gaze penetrating her. He was quite a good-looking fellow but that was irrelevant. She wondered if perhaps he was a friend of Paul's. It was only natural that she should respond for a split second; but it was at that precise moment, Paul caught her looking at the other man.

'Why are you looking at that man? Do you know him?'

Paul sounded agitated.

Pam was taken aback. She was lost for words.

'You know him don't you?' he said.

Paul was convincing himself there was a reason behind his wife's glance at that man.

'Don't be silly. I thought he was a friend of yours.'

Paul took another huge gulp of his lager and then got up. Pam was puzzled. No. Surely he wouldn't. But he did. At that moment, he swayed, slightly drunkenly over towards the man.

'Hey. Why are you looking at my wife? Take your bloody eyes off her.'

Pam was now deeply embarrassed. She could not believe Paul would do such a thing. The other man said nothing and tried to walk away. But Paul was having none of it. Pam had seen this happen so many times before. Why couldn't her husband control his obsessive jealousy?

'Come on you! Out with it! How well do you know her?'

Pam and Paul's friends were now fidgeting nervously. They'd seen it all before. But no-one got up to do something about his behaviour. Everybody at that table knew how violent Paul could be. None of them wanted to take him on. But, ultimately, it was Pam who would have to take some sort of action — and she would pay dearly for it later.

'Don't be so daft Paul. I've never seen him before in my life.'

'Liar. Fucking liar. I bet you've shagged him proper!'

'That's enough, Paul. Come on. Home. This is ridiculous.'

'I told you woman. Don't use those long words on me. Don't try and make me feel common.'

As the stranger disappeared into the crowded dance floor, Paul struggled to free himself of his wife's grasp. He hadn't finished his entertainment for that night by any means.

'You fucking slut. How dare you?'

The crunching sound of his fist sinking into her cheek was horrendous. Pam felt her teeth wobble as he connected with her face.

She crumpled to the floor, desperately holding her chin in place with her left hand. Too stunned to move. Too frightened to breath. Too terrified to utter a word. Then she heard it coming. A whoosh of air as his right hobnailed boot smashed straight into her shin as she lay there still trying to recover from his first flurry of punches. The crack was so loud it might well have broken the bone.

'Get your fucking clothes off you whore. You're just like a dog.'

That word 'dog' filled Pam with more pain and fear than the physical assault that had just occurred. It meant only one thing. He was going to degrade her like he had done so often before. She really did not know if she could take it again.

'Come on! Get those fucking clothes off *now*!'

Pam's favourite white dress that she had so lovingly washed and pressed just a few hours earlier was now ripped down the front exposing one of her breasts — brutally uncovered by her monster husband.

He walked over to the wardrobe next to their bed. It could mean only one thing. She felt the dread of expectation sinking through her mind and body. She knew the worst was still to come.

She had no choice. She was a prisoner in that bedroom yet again. She would have to do as he ordered. She had no option.

'I want everything off. Everything.'

Pam felt like a scared fox being pursued by one large, brutal hound. She scrambled along the floor and into the corner of the room and tried to sit up against the wall. But the pain was so severe, she could hardly move the leg he had so callously kicked just moments earlier. There was no escape.

Pam had already started to give up. She was

going to surrender once again. She started to remove her dress. In the end it was easier to rip it off. It took less time — that meant he would get it all over more quickly.

But getting her panties off was more difficult. Every time she tried to half get up to pull them off, she felt overcome by dizziness. But Paul Sainsbury was in no mood to be patient. His animalistic urges were taking full priority. He looked down at the pathetic creature who was his wife and grabbed one of her ankles before yanking the panties off. She could smell the awful stench of stale lager wafting from his lips. His eyes looked almost dead with alcohol as he staggered back to the wardrobe and pulled out various items.

'Come on dog. Come on. Behave like a dog. Be treated like one. You love it don't you? Don't you?'

Pam knew her husband was expecting her to reply. But her jaw and cheekbone were still vibrating from the throbbing pain inflicted by his punches minutes before.

'Come on. Say it. You dog.'

Pam looked up pathetically towards her towering brute of a husband.

'Woof. Woof.'

She could hardly spit the words out, the hurt was so bad. But Paul was satisfied. For the moment at least. He had lots more plans in store for his wife.

'Don't get up dog. I am going to take you for walkies.'

Paul then produced from behind his back a

collar and lead. Pam had seen it all before. She knew what to expect as he leant down and fixed the studded choker around her neck.

'You're a bitch and I am going to teach you a lesson. Dogs need training.'

Pam's brain was so scrambled by the onslaught that she had all but given up. That was the way he liked it. She just accepted her punishment — and provided him with the pleasure he so sickly craved.

Now she was on all fours being led around the bedroom by the lead. Every time she slowed down, he pulled viciously at the choker. She could feel her throat being pulled in. It was a bit like the sensation of drowning. She would snatch a few breaths and then he would yank viciously at the collar causing her neck to wrench.

Her husband had also now stripped naked. But he had only just begun. He was about to force his wife to perform some of the most degrading sex acts imaginable but first he wanted to make absolutely sure she really did feel like a dog.

'Come on eat. Eat I said.'

Paul Sainsbury put the dog bowl down on the floor by his wife's head. She did not know what was in the bowl. But just the smell of it made her feel nauseous. It could have been anything but it looked awful. Brown, splodgy pieces of something that filled the entire beige coloured bowl.

'Eat, I said. Eat.'

Pam crooked her neck downwards towards the bowl. She had no choice. If she did not eat it, he would beat her until she did. She may as well get it all over and done with as quickly as possible. This was a regularly recurring nightmare in the sad life of Pamela Sainsbury.

As her tongue probed the dark mess just in front of her tear-swollen eyes, she shut her mind out and began to eat.

Two hours had passed since that first punch. Now, at last, he had collapsed on the bed in a drunken stupor.

She had endured pain and penetration in virtually every orifice in her body. The spirit had been drained out of her but the frustration she was feeling was building up.

Pam struggled to get up off the floor. She fell back down at first. The dizziness brought on by her beating was so severe she could hardly balance herself. His cruelty towards her had known no bounds. She felt as if she had been raped, tortured and sodomised by a brutal attacker — not her own husband.

But through that haze of horror she felt a deep anger from within. Never again. Never again. Never again.

As she pulled at the leather studded choker that was still tightly wrapped around her neck, she felt a surge of disgust, fury and contempt for that animal lying there just a few feet away.

Throwing the collar and lead across the bedroom, she put on her dressing gown and sat for a few moments at the end of their double bed. This had happened over and over again. How could she just let him carry on? How many more times would she allow him to turn sex from an act of love into an act of aggression? Pamela Sainsbury had finally snapped. She was going to do something about it.

She washed her face and tried to straighten out her bedraggled appearance. Now was the time. She went to the tool cupboard at the bottom of the stairs of their modest three-bedroomed council house. She found Paul's work tool bag. In it was a long length of plumb line.

Back in the bedroom, Pam stopped and looked at the snoring hulk of a man who lay in their bed. He seemed so peaceful lying there. She had to make herself remember the disgusting degradation he had just put her through. This was the time to act. After eight years of abuse it had to be stopped.

Pam tied one end of the plumb line onto the headboard of their bed. Then she carefully and gently wrapped the rope fully around her husband's neck. He still couldn't feel a thing. The line was not tight — yet. He stirred at that moment. She thought perhaps she had disturbed him but it was only the restless sleep of a man pickled in alcohol.

Pam tightly wrapped both her small hands around the rope as if she were about to pull in a tug of war. She stood by the side of the bed with the rope coming towards her from her husband's neck. She took one last glance at his face. He was the man she had given up her entire life to be with. The man she had produced a family with. The man who actually probably really did love her in his own twisted, perverted way.

For a moment, she wondered if this really was the right thing to do. Perhaps he would change? Maybe there was a chance they could start all over again?

Pam knew there and then that would never happen. She had been through all this before. He had made promises and broken them all immediately. He wanted to love her to death. Now she had to kill him to avoid her own demise. There was no choice. With one huge heave, she pulled frantically at the rope. She could feel the strain on the headboard. It creaked as she tightened her grip. She also felt the rope burning into her palms as she pulled with all her strength.

Then he woke up. The very thing she most dreaded. He had shaken out of his drunken slumber as the rope dug deeply into his windpipe. She saw his eyes upon her. They were appealing, terrified eyes. The exact same look she had given him so often during the course of her beatings and abuse. Now he was suffering. He was experiencing the terror and the fear.

The moment his eyes opened she pulled even harder on the rope. It was as if his sheer agony was inciting her to accelerate the process of death. She could not stop herself now.

The colour was draining out of his face rapidly.

She could see the pupils of his eyes begin to dilate. His fingers had long since given up trying to grasp the rope away from his neck. His hands and arms had flopped down by the side of the bed. Pam somehow seemed to have found even more inner strength. The power she was generating was increasing. Nothing would allow her to let go of that rope until her job was complete.

The burning sensation caused by the rope digging into her hands had been replaced by deep set cuts in her skin. But she did not flinch. The pupils of his eyes had now completely dilated. There was just a flickering of white, nothing else. The eyelids were wide open though. It was as if they had been jammed open by some exterior force. Pam was glad his eyes were still open. It meant he had seen everything until the bitter end. That was important. That suffering had to continue for as long as possible.

With one last surge of energy, Pam gave one final tug.

But it was clear her husband was already well and truly dead. She relaxed her grip. Then his body seemed to convulse. Perhaps he was still alive? Maybe she had not completed the death sentence?

It seemed like an electric shock was running through his body for a split second. Pam was startled. She tried to regain her grip on that rope again. But by the time she had pulled it tight once more, her husband's body was still and limp. There was no life left inside him.

Now she had to remove him from the bed. He

had bludgeoned her body and mind for the last time. She had to be practical for a moment. She did not want her children, Lindsay and Terry to find their father like this.

Then Pam looked over at that wardrobe. It had become like an evil dungeon where he kept the whips, the collars, the leads and the other awful, perverted equipment that he had forced her to wear over the previous eight years.

Yes. He belonged in the wardrobe. There amongst the sick strands of leather and studs. Pam would make sure he was very comfortable there.

She untied the rope from the bed head and then noticed how deeply cut her hands had become. She went to wash down her hands before preparing to haul that dead piece of meat across the bedroom floor.

By the time she managed to push his body into that wardrobe, it was almost 3am. But it could have been any time of the day or night to Pam. She was caught up in the web of a fantasy that had become a reality. Had she really just killed her husband? Did she actually strangle the life out of him? Then, as if looking for some kind of reassurance, she glanced at the calendar by the side of their double bed — the bed where it had all just happened. And she wrote, words that soothed her tortured self, justified her actions, made sense of what had happened:

THIS IS THE FIRST DAY
OF THE REST OF MY LIFE.

It was September 1 1990 and Pamela Sainsbury's life had in fact begun all over again.

'He beat me up last night. Almost broke my leg. I told him to get out otherwise I'd call the police.'

Pam was very convincing as she told one of her husband's relatives why he was not at home.

'I think he's gone up north. I don't care anyway. I never want to see him ever again.' Only she realised that fact had already been guaranteed. None of the Sainsbury family or friends seemed that surprised. Some of them had witnessed his awful fit of jealousy at Carinas Nightclub a few days earlier. Paul was a brutal sort. Good riddance.

But while Paul Sainsbury had definitely gone for ever, he still presented something of a problem for his wife. Where could she put his body?

It was four days since his death and his lifeless remains were still stuffed in amongst his sex manuals and bondage equipment.

Pam decided that she had to do something. And once again, she was on her own. She could not afford to risk telling anyone.

Pam made one last check to see if the children were fast asleep. She crept into their bedroom and looked at their angelic faces for a few moments. It reassured her that all the horrors she had suffered had been worthwhile. Just to see them soundly sleeping was enough to convince her she had done the right thing. They were her flesh and blood and she wanted them to have the happiest lives possible. She would make sure of that.

Now that the house was quiet, she had to sort out the problem of Paul. She had to dispose of that body. But how? He was simply too heavy to carry out of the house in one piece. Pam removed a one foot long tenon saw and a razor-sharp carving knife from the kitchen and took them upstairs. She braced herself as she went to open the wardrobe — that evil mini-dungeon of horrors had got its just desserts now. The Master. The animal who inflicted such pain and anguish on Pam was now rotting amongst his own perverted possessions.

His stiff corpse fell out into the bedroom as she unlocked the double doors. The stench of death wafted out that instant. His naked body had turned a bluey-grey colour.

Pam held her breath for a moment. Some of the contents of his seized-up bowels were still in that wardrobe. It was a grisly sight for anyone to suffer. But Pam quickly recovered her composure. She had a job to do. She was not going to let him beat her — even in death. She would never again allow him the satisfaction of appalling her. She wanted to get away with the killing. She wanted to free herself from his evil spell. He was not going to force her into submission now — or ever again.

Pam rolled the heavy corpse of her husband over onto some plastic sheeting she had laid out on the floor of the bedroom. It was time to begin.

At first, it seemed really difficult to saw the arm

at the shoulder blade. The instrument just did not want to embed itself in the skin. Then Pam pressed down hard so that the razor sharp instrument sliced a niche in the soft bluey flesh. At last she could really get going.

Once she had conquered a certain technique with regard to the sawing, it was all relatively easy. Within a minute or two, the arm had been almost separated from the rest of the body. Pam gave it a slight tug and heard the final strands of flesh tearing as she pulled it off and laid it in a black dustbin liner. The only thing that surprised her was the weight. It was heavy. There was no way one could gingerly remove it. It definitely required a certain amount of strength and that made the whole process feel ever more real and graphic. Pam had envisaged it being much easier.

After depositing both arms in the plastic bag alongside the body, she moved down the corpse to begin work on the legs. They were even harder. Initially, she tried to cut them from where the thighs meet the stomach but that proved impossible. With a heave, she rolled the body over and began slicing through the hip bone.

More than an hour later, Pam had completed removing the the arms and legs from the torso. But there was still the matter of the head. She looked down at the cold, lifeless form on her bedroom floor and wondered if it really was Paul. Maybe he would come walking through that door at any moment? She sat there crouched on the plastic sheeting alongside what remained of her husband, in a sort of trance.

How can I be sure? How can I be certain he really is dead if I dispose of the body?

These questions were really troubling Pam. So long as his body had been rotting in that wardrobe she felt reassured that he was definitely dead. But now she was about to get rid of the body for ever. There would be nothing left of Paul — nothing to show her he really was dead.

She leant down and started to saw through his neck. By the time she had separated the head from the torso she had decided: she was going to keep his head. She wanted always to be absolutely sure he was actually dead.

It was way past midnight by the time Pam had hauled the two huge dustbin bags down to the back door. She hoped no one would see her when she began digging a hole near the vegetable patch at the end of the garden.

She took a shovel out of the garden shed and found what looked like a suitable spot and began digging. Well, she tried to dig. But the ground was as hard as a rock. There had been little rain for weeks and the earth was solid. No matter how much she crashed that shovel into the ground, only a few small clumps of earth moved.

She tried another part of the garden but it was much the same story. There was no way she could dig holes deep enough to bury those bags. Now she was getting worried that the neighbours in Le Lode

Close might see her out in the garden late at night and begin to wonder. No one had stirred yet. But if she made much more noise they were certain to get disturbed and then they would see what she was up to.

Pam returned to the kitchen, distraught. The remains of her husband in those two plastic bags were just sitting there by the back door. You can't get rid of me, they said in Paul's mocking voice, I've beaten you.

What could she do? He was not going to win. He just couldn't! She would think of another way of disposal.

Pam walked back down to the bottom of the garden and pushed her husband's wheelbarrow towards the back door. She struggled to load one bag at a time onto the wheelbarrow. The tension and turmoil of the previous few days was catching up with her. But any weakness was overcome when she thought about the driving force behind her actions. The quest to start a new life. That was enough to keep her going.

Pam was about to take an enormous risk but she had to get rid of the body. She weaved her way down the path to the back wall and ground to a halt. Then she summoned all her strength to heave the bag over the wall and into the the bushes that backed onto their house. It was thick bracken and a hedge that belonged to a field that never seemed to be used for anything in particular.

Pam repeated the operation with the next body

bag. She had got rid of the body the best way she could. She had got it off the premises — that was the most important thing.

Back in the kitchen, there was one bag remaining. It was smaller than the others. Round, shaped like a large football. That would stay at home, with pride of place in her cupboard, a perpetual reminder that he would not, could not, return.

The music was throbbing away as usual in Carinas Nightclub. But there was one big difference for Pamela Sainsbury. She was not living in fear of a severe beating the moment she got home.

For this was her first visit without her husband to the nightspot that marked the beginning and the end of her eight years of horror at the hands of a monster. As she relaxed near the busy bar with a girlfriend, she reflected on how — just a few weeks earlier — her life had all been so different.

She had stuck rigidly to that promise she made to herself the night Paul died. Every day she would look at the words written on her calendar: THIS IS THE FIRST DAY OF THE REST OF MY LIFE.

Now she was living the rest of that life and it was proving far more enjoyable than she would ever have believed. She could even afford to laugh and smile at men who caught her eye across the dance floor without facing that inevitable degradation. Soon she would feel confident enough to start going out with men again. Enjoying the company of, hopefully, gentler males than the sicko she had married.

But to start with she would keep them all at a bit of distance. It was going to take time to adjust back into the real world. For not only had she faced brutality beyond belief at the hands of Paul, but he had also forced her to spend most of her time trapped in that tiny house in much the same way the hostages were kept locked up in faceless parts of Beirut. She needed to adjust to normal, decent, hard-working people. But her girlfriends were proving a real mainstay.

They felt sorry for Pam. Abandoned by her bullying husband, she had been left to bring up the kids alone. She deserved to get out and have some fun occasionally.

By the time Pam and her friends left Carinas, they felt she was well on the road to recovery. But there was something nagging at her. A feeling that perhaps, just perhaps he was still around. Still watching over her. Still waiting for her to get home so he could batter her once again. Everywhere she looked there were reminders of him. This was his home town after all. It was an awful feeling. Just the slightest chance that he might not be dead. It sent a shiver of fear through her body.

There was only one solution. The moment Pam got home that evening she rushed through the hallway and pulled open the door to the tiny meter cupboard under the stairs.

It was OK. There was the shape of his head

pressing through the plastic bags she had tightly wrapped around it. She knew then that he was definitely dead. She had to keep his head as a constant reminder of her freedom. She stood there in the darkened hall for a few seconds and just stared straight at the grisly stump. She knew that no one must know what bizarre lengths she had gone to. But just so long as she knew, then it would be alright.

As the months passed by, Pamela gradually rediscovered her life once more. She learnt to enjoy herself. She started to date other men. She became a happier, more content person. And every time she felt any doubts or guilt about what she had done, she would return to that meter cupboard and make sure he was still there. The only really distressing aspect that still remained was the seclusion she felt whenever she faced his head there under the stairs. It was the only time she felt all alone in the world. She so desperately wanted to tell someone what had happened. Supressing the truth was not easy. There had been many times over the previous months when she had sat down in the kitchen of that same house — just a few feet from where Paul's lifeless face stood in the darkness — with a girlfriend and wondered to herself if she should talk about what happened on that awful night. Each time, she would hold herself back at the last moment, suddenly aware that it would be crazy to expect anyone not to tell the authorities.

But by the summer of 1991, Pam was reaching breaking point. She had to tell someone. She could not bottle it up any longer. She had managed to convince herself that by admitting it all to a friend it would then wipe out any of the remaining guilt once and for all. They say confession wipes the slate clean. Pam believed that her new life was perfect in all but one respect. It was time to tell.

'I am so relieved I've told you. It's so good to tell someone.'

Pam's girlfriend did not know how to respond. She was shocked and horrified by what she had just been told. Unfortunately for Pam, she had chosen the wrong friend to confide in.

'We'd like to talk to you about your missing husband.' The uniformed policeman standing on the front door of Pam's house seemed gentle enough in his approach. But she knew why he was there.

'Just give me a few minutes. I need to organise a babysitter for the kids.'

The officer was happy to wait while Pam went back inside the house. It gave Pam a chance to seek reassurance just one more time. She opened that meter cupboard door for the last time and looked in at him. It was enough. She knew for sure he was dead. He would never return. Now she felt a sense of relief that the police had come. It was perhaps the missing piece of the jigsaw. The one aspect that weighed on her mind. She had to confess to guarantee he never came back. Now the police were there she knew for certain he had gone. Calmly, she lifted the head of her dead husband and dropped it into her rubbish bin for the dustmen to take the next morning.

On Friday December 14 1991, Pamela Sainsbury was placed on two years probation after admitting the manslaughter of her husband Paul. She also pleaded guilty to a second charge of obstructing the coroner in his duty by concealing the body.

Plymouth Crown Court judge Mr Justice Auld told her: 'For many years you suffered regular and increasing violence and other forms of extreme sadism and sexual degradation at his hands. There is no right sentence in a case such as this. On one hand it is my duty to mark the serious crime of manslaughter which you have committed. However, I am prepared in the exceptional circumstances of this case to make a probation order for two years.'

The head of Paul Sainsbury was never recovered by police.

8

Slaughterhouse Lane

The sun had not yet risen above the fields of the picturesque village of Rosieres-aux-Salines. But the birds were already singing in the trees and the cattle were grazing peacefully on the green pastures that surrounded the sleepy hamlet.

The fruit trees in the garden of the white-washed cottage were carrying plentiful supplies of apples and pears that summer. Every now and again, a sparrow nestled its beak into a ripe piece of fruit, prompting it to drop to the ground where the insects feasted upon it.

A cock crowed from the distant farm across the fields, near the road where the cottage and a row of charming houses nestled neatly into the scenery.

That narrow route had the rather unnerving

name of Ruelle de L'Abattoir — Slaughterhouse Lane. Livestock from miles around was taken there to be chopped up into slabs of meat for a hungry public.

But now the slaughterhouse was no more. Only the name remained. The smell of rotting carcasses was just a distant memory to some of the village's older residents.

When the sun rose above the vast plains on clear June mornings like this, the white-washed houses gave off a wonderful warm orange glow before shimmering brightly as the day wore on.

The orchard that belonged to the cottage was flanked by well kept gardens filled with blue pine, dwarf juniper and beds of hydrangeas and zinnias.

Inside the house, Madame Simone Weber was stirred by the shrill of her alarm. It was 4.15am and she had a vital appointment to keep.

In fact she never really needed to bother with an alarm clock. For there had not been a day in her entire life when she did not wake up before it actually went off.

It was hardly surprising really. Madame Weber was a tense, highly strung woman of fifty six. She had seen much suffering during her life. Perhaps her soul wanted to make sure she never failed to rise each morning. At least that's what she told herself.

Madame Weber was a small, lumpy woman with watery eyes that stuck out from a gaunt face.

Her mouth was tight and hard with lips that looked like they hadn't received, or given, much love. A demeanour that did little to endear her to others. And yet, as the early morning puffiness around Madame Weber's eyes subsided, there was a hint of attractiveness about her. Something she used to her great advantage whenever she came across a possible suitor.

By 4.30am she was up and dressed in a white blouse and tweed skirt. It was an image that cut a respectable figure among the other residents of the village.

She looked out of the window at her garden. A beautiful sight in the low, golden sun.

But the splendour of the scene made no impression on Madame Weber. Her only concern was that appointment. It was a vital liaison. More important than any meeting she had ever planned in her entire life. She could not be late — no matter what.

As she got into her tiny green Citroen and started the engine, she didn't even notice the farmer from up the road waving good morning. He thought nothing of her rudeness. He was used to her strange behaviour and had come to accept it. In fact, he and the other locals preferred it that way. Most of them had refused to even acknowledge her existence after she inherited the house from her husband in 1980.

That might have seemed a heartless response — until you learned that she had only been married to eighty-year-old former gendarme Marcel Fixart for three weeks.

The marriage had scandalised the district. Local gossip had it that Madame Weber forced Fixart into a marriage he did not even realise had occurred.

The couple met through the lonely hearts column of a local newspaper. Madame Weber had once run a dating agency herself and knew just how vulnerable the people were who used their services.

Broke and virtually destitute, she decided that a brief relationship with an elderly man could be the answer to her problems.

She was only too well aware that her job at that time, as a washer woman, would hardly impress any prospective partner. So, before her first meeting with the old man, she bought herself a grey wig and renamed herself Monique Thuot — a retired professor of philosophy.

The relationship went slowly — far too slowly for Madame Weber's liking. She needed to marry Fixart to survive and he was reacting to her affections about as fast as a tortoise trying to climb the alps.

There was only one answer.

At the registry office in Strasbourg, it seemed like the fairy tale wedding of the elderly widower and the retired philosophy lecturer. But Fixart was back in Nancy — completely unaware of what was going on.

His place had been taken by aged retired actor Georges Hesling — paid a nominal sum by Madame Weber to act the part of Fixart.

It worked like a dream. To make matters even better both men died within weeks. No witnesses to the deception.

Fixart's family were outraged when they heard about the marriage *after* the old man's death. But there was nothing they could do about it.

When Madame Weber's survival plan had worked. She inherited £10,000 and a beautiful cottage. It was only years later that the truth emerged.

Her mind was still only on one thing — that appointment.

When Madame Weber's car slammed to a halt outside the gates of the battered looking factory on the edge of Nancy, none of the workers trooping in for the start of a hard day's work even looked up.

They were used to seeing the car. Madame Weber was a familiar face and they nearly all knew exactly what she was waiting for.

As the minutes passed by, she sat in her car, looking more and more irritated.

Just three yards away forty-eight-year-old factory foreman Bernard Hettier cowered behind a wall wondering what he should do.

He could see the Citroen in the distance. But luckily Madame Weber hadn't spotted him.

Bernard was a good looking guy in a very French, older man sort of way. He still had a good head of sandy coloured hair and he was slim with craggy, almost rock-like features.

In recent months, he had been studiously trying to avoid Madame Weber. It was all his fault really.

He should never have encouraged her into his bed in the first place. He should have known better. But his insatiable appetite for the opposite sex frequently led him into trouble.

Throughout two marriages, Bernard had found the lure of the flesh impossible to resist. He would often pick up vagrant women and seduce them before sending them packing. He loved them all: alcoholics, drifters, lost souls.

Like the time, only a few weeks earlier, when he met a dark-haired woman in a bar in Nancy. Bernard was sitting quietly sipping a beer when he caught her eye. At first she just looked away, slightly embarrassed by the attention. But he persisted and eventually swaggered over to her table. Few words passed between them. But Bernard was determined to get his way. Fifteen minutes later, he walked out of the bar with the woman, who was in her late forties. He always preferred them a bit older. They were far less complicated than the young ones. In his experience, the older women were more carefree — less obsessed with actual love. More interested in lust.

Less than one hour later the pair emerged from the tiny pension and waved coldly goodbye to one another having just made love.

He had an astonishing record of success. It seemed the Bernard Hettier school of charm really did work. And it was based on one simple theory: all women want to make love, whatever they might say at first. It was this principle that had attracted him to the distinctly unattractive Simone Weber in December, 1983.

She had called him after her lawn mower had broken down. A friend had recommended him highly. Madame Weber should have known how to fix it herself after her many years of experience as a car mechanic and restorer of old motors. But despite spending many hours tinkering with the engine, this lawn mower had her beaten — until Bernard appeared on the scene. Within minutes he got it going and was cutting the grass under the fruit trees in front of her cottage for the last time that winter.

For more than thirty minutes he trundled around the vast garden. She watched him fondly from a ground floor window as he did his job meticulously. Eternally grateful, she asked him in for a drink after all his efforts. It seemed only polite.

As she poured the bottle of beer for him, she felt a slight quiver in her stomach. Her hands shook with excitement. She couldn't take her eyes off him. He seemed so beautiful. Bernard sensed with his ever-delicate nose that sex was in the air.

As the drink began to work, altering perspectives and inhibitions, he studied her bulbous features and they began to look beautiful in their own unusual way. He could feel himself beginning to fall for this plump, matronly creature. Fatter women are always more sexy, he thought. They've got more to offer. He felt sure she was thinking along the same lines.

Just one hour later Bernard and Madame Weber were making hot, passionate love in her bedroom upstairs. The relationship had begun.

Now, he was cowering behind a wall in the factory, watching and waiting. Unsure whether to face the woman, whose obsessive love became so unbearable that he broke the rule of a lifetime and ended an affair acrimoniously.

Bernard had always used his easy-going nature and superb sense of humour to survive the onslaught of discarded women that littered his life.

He had such a relaxed attitude that it tended to rub off on his lovers. He was proud of the fact that even when he split with his lovers, it was always deemed by mutual agreement. Never acrimonious. Never nasty. Just civilised.

But then a lot of his women did not even know his full name, so it was not that difficult. Madame Weber was an exception to that rule — and it made Bernard feel uneasy. She also happened to know there was no other exit to that factory on that day. She was quite content to pass the time. Her lover was going to have to come through those gates — no matter what.

She seemed blissfully unaware that Bernard was a less than willing participant in this game of romance. He might have told her in no uncertain terms that it was over because he was seeing another woman, but she had steadfastly refused to accept the notion. She needed Bernard desperately. She longed for his body and his company. He made her feel young in a way no other man had ever done.

She was desperate for that physical contact. The emotion. The touching. The sex.

'It's no good. I am going to have to face her,' thought Bernard to himself that morning.

He could not cower there for the rest of the day. He was exhausted from a gruelling ten hour night shift at the factory. And now this.

Bernard braced himself, took a deep breath walked towards the factory gate. He knew that Madame Weber would spot him within seconds but he steeled himself to look only dead ahead. 'She'll get the message if I don't look her in the eyes,' he thought. He couldn't have been more wrong.

Madame Weber was elated. There was Bernard. He looked tired but what did that matter? All she saw were his handsome features. There was a sensuous, warm feeling in her stomach. Like getting butterflies but far more forceful. She knew at that point she loved Bernard. Those were the vital signs.

Bernard sneaked a glance to his right to try and make out whether she had stirred from the Citroen. He didn't want to look her in the face.

He hesitated for a moment, taken aback with surprise. The car was empty. Where was she? Perhaps it wasn't her car. Relief flooded back into his body.

Suddenly, a hand grasped him from behind.

'Bernard. It's so good to see you. We must talk.' His heart sank.

The tension returned instantly. Why couldn't

she just leave him alone?

How could he get away from her? He was her emotional prisoner.

The worst part of it for Bernard was the temptation. Months ago, he had wanted to get rid of this woman from his life forever. But now he was near her, he knew it would be virtually impossible to resist her. The physical need was always in him. Lurking. Just waiting for an opportunity. No matter how much he told himself he hated her, he wouldn't be able to stop himself.

But he truly wished she was not there in the first place.

So far, Bernard had responded with nothing more than a cursory 'Oh hello.'

But that was enough. He had caved in. He had accepted her presence.

He was her captive. Emotionally and physically. Sometimes he would black out in her living room for no apparent reason. It would always happen just as he was about to leave after giving her the promised dose of passion she so actively pursued.

Bernard always wanted to get out of that house the moment they had completed the act. The feeling of guilt and disgust would sweep over him as she lay there in her layers of middle-aged fat, looking longingly into his eyes. He would turn away in horror and promise himself, 'Never. Never again.' But he always came back for more.

After fainting, he would wake up in her bed and She would be nursing him back to health. Tending to him so lovingly. Spoon feeding him medicine she said would make him feel better. And he would be eternally in her debt. He couldn't just get up and walk out. It would be so rude so he'd stay there a little longer, duty bound to perform once more.

As if his dizzy spells weren't enough, he'd recently been plagued by regular lapses of memory. On a number of occasions he would completely forget arrangements that had been made after going out with Madame Weber.

Sometimes he would make love with her and find himself slipping into a trance-like state. Losing track of time and staying far too long in her company. His friends began to complain about his unreliability. Why was he always late after he had been with her?

He began to wonder whether she was doing something to him to ensure that he became her prisoner, whenever she wanted him. But it seemed a ludicrous notion. However, it got really serious when he started falling asleep at his desk in the factory. On one occasion, he was almost fired by his boss when he was discovered slumped over the bureau.

He went for tests at the local hospital and the doctors suggested he was perhaps being drugged by someone. At the time he hadn't really clicked. Who would want to do that? And why?

Now, as he stood outside the factory gates with the one woman in the world he had no wish to ever see again, he reckoned he knew the answer.

'Let's go to your home. We must talk,' insisted Madame Weber.

Once again. Bernard didn't need to bother replying. This was an order not a request. There was no point in arguing.

As they drove the three miles to his modest home along twisting hedged-line lanes, he thought about the last time she had caught him outside the factory gates. How he had sworn he wouldn't let her cast her spell on him ever again.

That was a few weeks ago. And here he was, weak as ever.

As the couple pulled their cars up alongside the flat fronted house, all was still deadly quiet in the neighbourhood. It was still only 6.30 in the morning but in preparation for the long day ahead Bernard Hettier felt as if his day was over.

Inside the house, Madame Weber's warmness returned — the feeling she had enjoyed so many times when they had been regular lovers. Before she had had to become much more forceful.

She remembered the love they had shared inside the slightly tatty bedroom with its worn, cream coloured walls. At first he had been so energetic, so innovative. He'd brought her to unbelievable peaks of ecstasy.

She made them both a cup of coffee while Bernard wondered to himself how he ever got himself into this messy affair. What on earth drove him to seduce this roly-poly shaped woman? And then expect to just walk away from the relationship. It was obvious she would come after him. How could she — the plain ex-nurse turned motor mechanic — accept that it was all over? She had nothing else. No one to love her. *He* was alright. There were always women around for him. But she had no prospects of companionship other than him.

He should have thought of that when they met in her garden on that very first occasion.

Now, as they sat making difficult, almost stiff conversation, it finally dawned on Madame Weber that he was trying to get away from her for good.

There was a certain deadness about his responses towards her. That wouldn't do. It wouldn't do at all. She must make sure there was no escape for him. He wasn't going to discard her like some used car. Not this time. It had happened to her so many times before.

She had put up with his philandering. The constant flow of other women. She even recalled the day she arrived at his house unexpectedly only to find him performing an unspeakable act. What hurt so much was that it was with some waif and stray, another woman was even older than her.

Then again, it excited her to realise what a sexual animal he was.

Bernard was starting to feel slightly queasy. He presumed it was the fact he had been working all night was taking its toll.

He watched Madame Weber sitting opposite

him at the coffee table but she was gradually slipping out of focus.

Then he blinked and his vision of her was cruelly sharp once more.

Her mouth spouted disjointed words that jabbed in the air. 'How's work going? Holiday. Holiday. You, really …' They seemed like solid objects so that everytime they entered his head they bounced around him.

Then his brain awaiting recognition began to drop. Sleep — gorgeous, welcoming sleep was all he needed. He jerked his head up again and just managed to recover consciousness.

He never woke up again.

Madame Weber had a lot of strength in her fat-enclosed muscles. She'd acquired it through her work restoring and fixing vintage cars in her Nancy garage.

She needed every tiny bit of that power to help Bernard from her car to her sister's tiny apartment in the noisy Avenue de Strasbourg in the heart of the bustling city.

He wasn't conscious but somehow she managed to make him look like just another late afternoon drunk as she struggled up the stairs to the third-floor flat in the four-storey Victorian house.

She was driven by a hard determination to settle her love for this suburban-style Don Juan once and for all. This was the ultimate test that she had to pass. It would be a true insight into how much she really cared for him.

Jean Haag and his wife Marie were both in their eighties and had been residents on the ground floor of that very same building for forty years. They knew Madame Weber and her sister Madeleine reasonably well in a neighbourly sort of way.

The Haags were very steeped in their own ways. They couldn't cope with new-fangled contraptions like television. But the preoccupation that kept them alive more than anything else was a healthy inquisitiveness for all that went on around them. There wasn't a thing that went on in that house or the street outside, they didn't know about.

Frequently they would view the comings and goings from their front window, just by the only steps into the building, or peep through the spy-hole in their door if they heard anyone coming up or down the hallway.

They didn't need television. They had a round-the-clock live show featuring real people instead.

One of their favourite subjects was Madame Weber and her activities. She really intrigued them. Sometimes she would burst through the hallway doors late at night to stay the evening at the apartment. On other occasions she would spend entire days entertaining men friends above them and the Haags would listen, puzzled to the bumps and the squealings. It was a long time since they'd used a bed in that way.

They couldn't help noticing Madame Weber on

that afternoon. After all, she did seem to be helping a rather drunken male friend into the house.

Madame Haag watched intently at the window while Weber struggled to find the key. Then her husband spied through the peep hole in their door as the couple slumped through the hallway.

They never saw him come down again.

Upstairs, Madame Weber was making a hell of a racket. Bernard was now flat out on the floor of the living room. She felt his pulse. It was weak. She began tearing up black plastic bin liners and spreading them flat next to Bernard, tucking them under his back every now and then.

In the corner of the room lay a huge concrete cutter. It was a mean, unforgiving piece of hardware in every sense of the word. It seemed oddly out of place. In the room next door lay two .22 rifles, a silencer and three sticks of dynamite. She grimaced gleefully.

This was the sweet climactic moment. Ever since he had broken off what she saw as their engagement, she had been building up to it. She always hoped they could get together again. But she knew that it was not to be.

She kept thinking of how happy she had been when they were true lovers. Much happier than she had ever been before.

How she survived a first marriage that produced five children God only knows. Her husband had been a quiet, stoic man called Jaques Thuot. But his calmness was soon countered by the sheer dominance of Madame Weber.

It was a marriage that M. Thuot described as 'living hell.'

Not exactly helped by the fact that she got him committed to a mental hospital after pretending he had tried to kill her.

It was the ultimate revenge on a husband whose only sin was to seek a quiet life without the emotional upheaval that was a part of Madame Weber's staple diet.

When M. Thuot was committed to a real strait-jacket environment it was, as he later explained, 'like going from one version of hell to another.'

And what of those five children? The unstable nature of her own life rubbed off on them with heartbreaking consequences. One daughter committed suicide in her teens. The reasons were never really uncovered. The son she so doted on was sent away to Germany on national service. He also took his own life — because he could not bear to be parted from the mother he so desperately loved.

That was before the farcical second marriage that was never consummated. Then along came Bernard. But he proved to be as bad as all the others. Actually, in many ways, he was even worse.

At least the others were faithful, if somewhat unlikely creatures.

Now she was planning a future where he would

always be in her thoughts. If she could not have him then no one else would get him.

She always knew she had it in her to kill. She had to prove it.

The saw turned slowly at first when she switched it on. But it rapidly gained such speed that it was impossible to make out the serrated edge of the blade.

The man in the equipment hire shop the previous morning had warned Madame Weber that the saw was really built for men to handle.

She was outraged. She had handled much larger bits of equipment over the years. How dare he suggest she wasn't fit for the job. She would show him.

Women are just as strong as men when they really want to be. Men always think they are supreme. They need to be taught a lesson.

But all the same she heeded his advice when he warned: 'It's very dangerous. Handle it with care, or it'll slice your finger off just like that.'

It sounded perfect.

Back in the flat, Madame Weber heaved up the heavy saw.

Protected by a brand new plastic fronted apron and wearing skin tight black rubber gloves, she knelt down and tweaked the whirring blade against Bernard's flesh. It was surprising how little resistance it met.

The incision was sharp and precise. Her hand

trembled with excitement before she swept the cutter across his chest. It was so easy, the blood burned as it met the hot metal while sealing the flesh as she went along. Soon he would be in nice square slabs. She'd be able to handle him quite easily then. Oh yes indeed.

Downstairs, the Haags could not help but notice the sound of what they presumed was one of those vacuum cleaners. It seemed a slightly strange noise for a vacuum cleaner to make. But what did they know?

Madame Weber was now beginning to appreciate why concrete block carving was considered by some to be an art form.

Every time she sliced into another portion of Bernard's body she felt an exquisite rush of adrenalin to her brain. The patterns she could make were so pretty. It was so nice of Bernard to continue to provide her with so much pleasure.

She had severed his arms and legs from the torso with ease. It had been a bit like cutting up a chicken after it had been cooked. Now, she had to remove the head. That might be a little difficult. With the blade still whirring furiously she knelt down and held the throbbing machine over his jugular vein.

It had to be neat and tidy. Putting the body on plastic bin liners had worked perfectly. It had prevented the blood from seeping through to the floor below.

As the blade sliced through the throat, she waited for the blood to spurt, but it just came out in a steady, manageable stream.

Within a minute, the entire head had been decapitated. Her pudgy fingers grasped the head by its hair. It was remarkably heavy. For a second she feared she might drop it. But soon it was wrapped up safely in a heavy duty plastic bag. She had bought thirty of them at the same time as hiring the saw.

It was to hide the head from view. It was the one aspect of the dissection she had found faintly distasteful. But there was still work to do — a massive spring clean. She couldn't leave her sister's apartment in a mess. It would be so inconsiderate …

'You have got to help. We know he's in danger. This woman was very strange. He told us she always had a pistol with her, day and night.'

Bernard's sister Monique Goetz was frantic with concern for her missing brother as she stood in Nancy Police Station, pleading for help. Her appeal was falling on deaf ears. The police had heard it all before.

A self-confessed romeo goes missing, leaving behind a long list of women he has loved and left.

'So what's new?' asked the cynical policemen behind the desk at the station.

Here was a man known for his sexual liaisons with hundreds of women and the police are supposed to sit up and take immediate action? He knew what had happened. Good old bonking Bernard Hettier had arranged his own disappearance to start a new life somewhere else, probably with a new lover.

Back at the tiny flat, Madame Weber was struggling out of the house with plastic bag after plastic bag. The Haags were fascinated. They had never seen so many bags left out for the rubbish collection in one go.

On the fifth load, Madame Weber felt a pang of panic when she noticed a gaping hole opening in the side of one bag. His head might fall out! She rushed to the bin just in time.

By the time the seventeenth and very last bag had been disposed of, Madame Weber felt a weird mixture of relief and exhaustion.

Inside the flat she opened up a suitcase Bernard had left at the flat many months previously, after one of their romantic interludes. It seemed the perfect place to to put his torso. In the end, in Madam Weber's eyes at least, he had brought about his own downfall. Now his own suitcase was going to carry his remains to their last resting place at the bottom of the River Marne. His remains would be weighted to the river bed by a slab of concrete from the garden he so lovingly mowed all that time ago. She wanted him to feel the full weight of her fury dragging him down, even after death.

Her sister Madeleine and her nephew had virtually volunteered their assistance in covering up his disappearance. They felt duty-bound to help this poor, much maligned woman.

'He's gone away for a while. He doesn't want to be bothered. He'll get in touch when he feels the time is right,' the male voice on the phone was hesitant, nervous.

On the other end of the line was Bernard's latest lover — the woman who had ultimately lured him away from Madame Weber. She was stunned. How could Bernard just get up and run away? They hadn't argued. There had been no hints of discord.

She felt angry and betrayed. His behaviour was outrageous. But, her friends told her, that was the sort of man she was dealing with.

The blurred voice, who described himself as Bernard's friend, was adamant. He would not be back for a long time. A very long time.

At the factory where he worked, the boss was hardly surprised to receive a Paris doctor's medical certificate stating that Bernard was too ill to work. Madame Weber's loyal nephew took care of that by posing as Bernard in the French capital city — a long way from Nancy. His stomach pains were so realistic, the doctor warned him to go to hospital if they persisted.

It might be some time before Bernard would be returning to work again.

At the equipment hire shop, the attendant was in a dismissive mood, muttering to himself 'Typical woman. She goes and gets that concrete cutter stolen. She should never have hired it in the first place. It's a man's machine.'

Just moments earlier, Madame Weber had bitten her lip and held her temper after the man had mocked her when she returned to the shop to pay for the stolen item. She knew she shouldn't create a scene. She wanted her visit to that shop to be as low key as possible.

Madame Weber parked outside a row of garages near her sister's villa in Cannes. This was where they would hide Bernard's rickety old car. Her sister, a dark haired version of herself in almost every way, pulled open the garage doors and Madame Weber drove the car straight into the opening.

As she slammed the garage doors shut she was overcome with relief. Yet another part of that man's life had been locked away. Soon there would be nothing left of him in the entire world. The two sisters walked away and Madame Weber turned and warned Madeleine, 'We must be careful. People will be watching us. Listening to our every word.'

It proved to be a chillingly correct statement.

Back in Nancy, Bernard's family were very persistent. They wouldn't rest until an investigation was launched.

'He may have been a lady's man. But he wouldn't just disappear off the face of this earth. Something has happened to him. You have to help.'

Eventually, the police accepted that this was no everyday disappearance.

There was only one person the gendarmes could turn to — Judge Gilbert Thiel.

The bearded, bespectacled former lawyer was, under French law, the man who would have to head the investigation — and find out if there were any suspicious sides to the enquiry. His correct, formal title was Juge d'Instruction, or examining magistrate, a position with no equivalent in the British system of justice.

In principle, his duty was to gather all possible facts to relating to the matter in hand, weigh them with the proper objectivity and deploy his powers accordingly in deciding whether or not a case can proceed.

The appeals from the family were growing and Judge Thiel knew something had to be done — and Bernard's sister Monique was adamant that Madame Weber was involved.

'It is completely within her powers. She is a strange woman. Mad enough to do it. I know she's involved.'

Judge Gilbert had a hunch she might be right. Whatever the situation, he had little else to go on, so he launched the investigation by ordering a phone tap on Weber and her sister Madeleine.

'Do you think we should find a new school for Bernadette?' Madame Weber was talking on the phone from her cottage to her sister in Cannes.

They weren't discussing a child as one might presume. They were talking about the car. It was their cryptic code word for it. The 'school' was the garage.

Madame Weber was worried. She had heard strange clicking sounds on her phone for weeks.

She was pretty sure she was under surveillance but she had no hard and fast evidence.

Then she got a phone call from the estate agent who rented her the garage.

'Mme Chevalier. Do you wish to renew this monthly agreement?' he asked.

The officers listening to this were intrigued. Suddenly, some of those missing pieces of the jigsaw were starting to come together.

Judge Thiel and his officers soon traced the garage to Mme Chevalier. Weber had been using a false name and they were on to something. Anybody who uses a false name has something to hide.

The garage door was not difficult to force. The Cannes police were somewhat bewildered by the request of their colleagues in Nancy, but they understood it was a murder investigation so they cooperated.

Inside the tatty lock-up they found Bernard's Renault 4. Now Thiel was beginning to understand Weber's cryptic telephone conversations.

But the car in itself was not enough to prove Madame Weber was involved in the murder of Bernard. They needed more evidence. Much more.

For she had a left an intricate trail of deception

across France in a desperate bid to avoid implication.

Judge Thiel was stunned. He had just burst into the tiny apartment on the Avenue de Strasbourg hoping to find some traces of human flesh or maybe even some blood on the floor. Instead he had found nothing to connect Madame Weber with Bernard Hettier's mysterious disappearance.

Then, as the officers casually looked in the room next door, they uncovered an arson that more befitted the safe house of an international terrorist than a grandmotherly widow. He was staring straight into the barrels of two .22 rifles, a silencer, three sticks of dynamite in an old handbag and in a casserole pot in the kitchen, 40 rubber stamps stolen from town halls, local government offices and chemists' shops.

It was an astounding haul — and it put matters in a completely different perspective.

But he still had found no trace of a body.

The children playing on the edge of the River Marne, just south of Paris, thought it was their lucky day. They had spotted a suitcase washed up on the bank and were trying to open it.

They didn't bother to think why a breeze block was attached to the handle in order to make it sink without trace. And they wouldn't have known that the blue dab of paint on the stone was the same colour and brand as the freshly painted blue gable of that cottage in Slaughterhouse Lane.

As they grappled with the lock to try and force it open, a man walking on the river bank waved them away. He instantly knew that this was not hidden treasure.

The policeman who eventually forced open the case vomited on the spot. Inside was a torso without head, arms, or legs. In Nancy, Judge Thiel reckoned he had the body of Bernard Hettier.

On November 8, 1985, he and three officers turned up at the white-washed cottage in Rosieres-aux-Salines and arrested Simone Weber.

For more than five years — the longest period of remand ever instituted — Madame Weber was kept in custody without facing her accusers as Judge Thiel continued, some said obsessively, to gather evidence that would conclusively prove the crimes she had committed.

On March 1, 1991, Simone Weber, by now aged 60, was found guilty of the brutal murder of her lover Bernard Hettier and sentenced to 20 years in prison.

In one of the most sensational trials in French legal history, she was also acquitted of the murder of her second husband Marcel Fixart for lack of evidence.

The newspapers labelled her the She-Devil of Nancy, and it stuck.

9

Car Ride to Hell

Shopping malls are virtually an institution throughout the United States of America. They are vast spreads of stores all in one place with just one car park. Very convenient. Very cosy. Very safe.

The idea behind them is that shoppers can get everything they want in one place. It saves time — and time is money.

The Puente Hills Mall, in California's San Gabriel Valley was a typical example. Despite being just 25 miles from the centre of sprawling, glamorous Los Angeles it could have been one of a thousand such malls stretched across the nation.

At any one moment there would be hundreds of vehicles parked in the vast car park in front of the main entrance to the Puente Hills Mall. Mothers with their children. Husbands with their wives. Grandparents with their grandchildren. Every cross section of the local population. The rich. The not so rich. The poor. The not so poor. They all had one thing in common — a need to shop, a need to buy — and Puente Hills was the perfect location.

Besides every type of store, there were banks, estate agents, restaurants and, naturally, a MacDonalds. Basically, shopping malls like the one at Puente Hills were the classic example of the American Dream. Stores competed with each other to keep prices rock bottom. Huge advertising hoardings blared out at you the moment you drove into the car park. It was a place where you could spend all your hard earned cash, but still feel you were getting good value for money.

Robbin Machuca, Eileen Huber and John Lewis looked every inch the products of that American Dream as they sat in Eileen's brown Mercury car at the Mall on August 27, 1991.

Robbin and John were half-brother and sister. Her darker skin contrasting with the lighter brown features of John. Eileen was Caucasian — the product of a one-parent middle class family in a cosy nearby suburb. But the racial mix of the group hardly raised an eyebrow in the mall on that day. This was not the Deep South in the 1930s. This was California in 1991 — blacks and whites had long since learned to befriend each other without fear of retribution.

But then you wouldn't think so if you met

Eileen's father Gary. He was known as 'John Wayne' in the neighbourhood where they lived because of his vast collection of guns. But other, less kind, souls called him 'White Trash' or 'Redneck' because he still hinted at believing in white supremacy.

Though overpowering, his attitudes had not rubbed off on 20-year-old-Eileen. Her fiancé John was black and she was proud of it. Maybe she was also secretly quite pleased that her father so disapproved.

Eileen loved being in the company of John and Robbin. They had such a laid back attitude towards life. 'Live for the day, for tomorrow may never come.' They worshipped that famous line written by Jimi Hendrix. It encompassed their feelings about the world.

You see, so many tragedies had already befallen John, aged 21, and Robbin, aged 26. Their lives were like a web of endless disasters, one outrage leading to the next. Long ago, their American Dream had turned into an American Nightmare. John's mother was an alcoholic, his father a pimp shot dead on the mean streets of South Central Los Angeles when he was a baby.

As a small boy he would throw rocks at the family's German Shepherd dog until one day the dog broke its chain and mauled him viciously. At just eight years of age, he was arrested for armed robbery. By the time he was 10, he was in a juvenile detention centre. Then he joined one of the city's most notorious gangs — the Westside Bloods. It was his escape from anonymity. Now he was a person in his own right. He had an identity at last. A reputation as a cruel, violent gang member. But at least they knew who he was.

Then he met Eileen Huber.

John's half sister Robbin could give a pretty similar account of her background. Her father was an American Indian in jail for armed robbery when she was born. At 12 years of age, she became pregnant by her stepfather. Confused and afraid she denied it at first. Even as the doctor delivered the baby, she told her stepfather: 'You're lyin'. You cannot be the father.' But he knew it was true.

A few months later, Robbin's stepfather confessed his evil deed to his wife. He handed her mother a gun and ordered her to shoot them all. Her mother refused. But, to her daughter's eyes, she committed the ultimate act of betrayal by refusing to kick her husband out of that house. Bitter and hysterical, Robbin grabbed the baby and jumped out of the back window of their home. She never came back. She joined the gangs. She did hundreds of burglaries. At 15 she was jailed. It was a blessing in disguise. At last, Robbin had a place to rest her head. A place to learn. She was taught secretarial skills. On her release she got a job in a mortgage company. Her probation officer was convinced she had escaped her tragic background and could start afresh. Robbin seemed happy. But then there came a turning point. Her apartment was wrecked by burglars in just the same sort of crime she used to commit. She could not cope with the losses. Robbin quickly returned to her old, familiar ways.

It all made Eileen's family history pale into insignificance. Until very recently she had lived in the same house all her life. Even her freckle-faced strawberry blonde looks had hardly altered since early childhood. She was so skinny they used to call her Olive Oyl, after Popeye's girlfriend.

All the other kids used to love going around to her house because it was like an Aladdin's cave of film star fantasy. On the lounge walls were posters of John Wayne, her father's hero. But Eileen's room was like a shrine to her favourite idol Lucille Ball. When people walked in, they felt they were entering a time warp back to the fifties. Pictures of the blonde comedian adorned every inch of wall space. She'd always loved Lucy. They used to say she was just like her. And that made Eileen feel good. On the book shelves were videos of every movie Lucille Ball ever made. They were crammed between countless novels with titles like Miss Teen Sweet Valley.

But Eileen started to question her life just a year earlier. She had begun to wonder what future lay ahead. The outlook was bleak. It felt empty and meaningless. Written in red felt tip pen on the wall above the headboard of her bed was a nagging piece of graffiti dated July 25, 1990. 'What's come over you?' The adolescent scrawl begged. 'Help me somebody … please.'

Eileen's father Gary never even bothered to read it. Now these three desperate people seemed to be putting on a brave face as they laughed and smiled whilst chatting between mouthfuls of tasty Chinese food in the Puente Hills Mall on that day in August, 1991.

'Don't you care about anything?'

Eileen was laughing as she uttered those words. But there was a serious undercurrent to what she was asking her friend Robbin.

'I'd rather not care than care 'cuz then you get hurt.' Robbin's reply summed it all up really. She was dead inside. She had felt like that for so long she reckoned there was nothing left to lose. Life had dealt far too many blows in her direction. What could she possibly owe to anyone? No one had given her anything but pain. To care would be like paying back a debt that she didn't owe …

Just a mile away at the Lynx Golf company, 56-year-old Shirley Denogean was leaving her firm's offices for her lunch break. She usually bought a sandwich at one of the nearby cafés but on this particular day she had to buy a birthday card for a relative.

The easiest place to find one was at the Puente Hills Shopping Mall. And Shirley was a regular at the Mall — it was her favourite place to hunt for bargains. In any case, it was a beautiful hot sunny day in the San Gabriel Valley. Perfect for a short drive.

As Shirley turned on the ignition of her silver 1980 Mercedes, her only thoughts were on buying that card and getting back to work on time. She did not want to upset her bosses by taking an extra long lunchbreak. At first the car did not start. But then it was always doing that. Shirley tried again. This time the vast V8 engine came to life. If only it hadn't.

'She's perfect.'

John Lewis spat out the words between heaps of Chinese food stuffed in his mouth. All three of them were watching Shirley Denogean driving her Mercedes into the parking lot at the Puente Hills Shopping Mall.

'Let's wait until she comes back.'

The two women giggled nervously in anticipation as Lewis barked his order at them. They all knew what was about to happen. This wasn't the first time.

Inside the greetings card shop, Shirley looked at her watch slightly anxiously. The drive had taken longer than she expected. She had to be back at the office in a few minutes. After paying the cashier, she walked briskly back to her gleaming, spotless car. There was no time to waste. In her haste, she did not see Lewis and the two women approach. There were so many people around that day. There was nothing unusual about a black couple and a white girl. Why should she notice them?

'Get in the fucking car — now!'

Shirley Denogean felt a sharp stabbing pain as the barrel of Lewis' gun prodded deep into her back. For a split second she felt annoyed that anyone should come anywhere near her. How dare they? They must have made a mistake. This could not be happening to her, surely?

But the reality of the situation rapidly dawned on Shirley when she turned around and saw the blank, emotionless faces of her assailants and then looked down and saw the gun pointing towards her.

'I said in the car, bitch!'

This time Shirley did exactly what she was told. She felt her stomach tighten inside, like somebody had grabbed it then twisted. She wanted to heave through fear, but there was absolutely nothing she could do. To anyone walking by, it would have seemed like a perfectly ordinary scene. Four people sitting in a saloon car about to drive off. If they had looked more closely, they would have seen the horror on the face of Shirley Denogean. They would have sensed the robber's adrenalin pumping, seen the pupils in the eyes dilating through nervous excitement.

'What do you want? Have anything.'

Shirley began ripping open her purse. Cash and credit cards cascaded onto the floor of the Mercedes. She looked at the faces of those two women. She wondered how they could do this. She understood a man but not the women? Surely they must feel some empathy for another female? But there was nothing there for Shirley to grasp at. Robbin and Eileen had done this before. This was just another 'job' — they would not have even known what the word empathy meant. She had money and that was all that mattered.

'Give me the fucking number NOW! Or we'll kill you, mother fucker!'

Lewis grasped hold of the bank cash card and

yelled at Shirley. He seemed out of control. Almost on a terror trip. His head felt filled with blank spaces. There was no feeling. There was no sorrow. There was no pity. He just wanted the password for that card so he could steal her money.

Shirley watched helplessly as Eileen Huber walked off towards the ATM machine just a few yards from where they were parked. Beside her in the back seat of her own Mercedes was Robbin Manchuca. In front, Lewis. She wanted to scream her head off to alert one of the hundreds of people walking nearby. But she feared they might use that gun if she so much as uttered a word out of place.

This was a battle for survival for Shirley. And pride. Your dignity is the first thing that goes when fear grips you and won't let go. She tried to remain calm but the tears of terror were welling up in her eyes. She felt close to bursting point. But she wasn't going to let them get her. She had to be hard. She did not want to show them her emotions. That would give them instant victory. She did not want them to win.

Shirley looked closely at Robbin. She had an attractive, almost soft face. How could this woman even contemplate the crimes they were participating in? Surely they would not kill her? Not two women? There had to be some mercy there. There had to be some understanding.

By the time Eileen returned from the cash dispenser, the atmosphere had relaxed somewhat.

Few words had been exchanged between any of those people in that car.

But something was about to happen. She could sense it. Her hands were sticky with sweat. She felt the silence on them and the air was so thick she could hardly breath

Robbin stepped out of the Mercedes after Eileen got back in. What was happening? Perhaps they were going to leave her now? Shirley prayed that this was the end of her nightmare. Tragically, it had only just begun.

Lewis started up the car. Just like earlier it did not turn over first time. For the first time in her life Shirley wished her car would conk out completely. Behind them, Robbin had started Eileen's Mercury first time. She waited for her step-brother and his fiancée to get going. After a few agonising seconds, the Mercedes roared into life.

Then followed a bizarre trip around all the cash dispensers that existed in Puente Hills Shopping Mall. Each time Lewis spotted one he would carefully pull the car to a halt in a parking space and prod the barrel of his revolver into Shirley's side.

'What's the number for this fucking card? What is it?' Shirley had a lot of cash cards in her purse that day — it was like a windfall to Lewis and the two women.

Robbin's boyfriend Vincent Hubbard had been absolutely right when they had discussed a good way of making fast bucks.

'Hit the cash dispensers, man,' he'd said. 'It's fucking easier than holding up liquor stores. Fewer witnesses. Less problems.'

Hubbard would have been there with them that day if he hadn't volunteered to stay home with Robbin's five-year-old daughter. But then Hubbard should have known. He had just got out of jail after serving time for everything from robbery to drugs. Cash card dispenser hold-ups were the talk of the cells in the LA County Prison.

Now Lewis, Robbin and Eileen were cleaning up as much cash as they could from Shirley Denogean's credit cards. It was a horrific ride for her. The longer it went on the more certain she was that they were going to kill her. The more money they got the more brazen they became. By the time they had taken cash out of a sixth machine, Lewis and the two women were positively oozing excitement.

'This is fucking great. We won't have to do another job for weeks.'

Lewis was ecstatic. All this cash was like a gift from God.

'Hey John. We're goin' to have ourselves a real good time.'

Eileen was looking forward to a few weeks without the usual money problems. Robbin — following behind in the Mercury — was happy too. None of them gave a moment's thought to the terrified middle-aged woman they had just kidnapped and taken on a ride to Hell.

They had run out of cash dispensing machines.

Now this horrible convoy of death was about to begin its final journey.

'Let's head for the freeway.'

Lewis knew that the nearby motorway was the best route out of the Puente Hills Shopping Mall. If anything did go wrong then they could be away and on the main road in seconds. Shirley Denogean knew what it meant as well. She was convinced it meant the beginning of the end of her life.

'Go ahead. Kill me now.'

Lewis looked around the moment he heard Shirley utter those words.

'What the fuck …? Shut the fuck up will ya?'

Eileen looked away almost embarrassed by their captive's outburst and her lover's reply. But it was only a momentary lapse — she worshipped the very ground John Lewis walked on. She could see no evil in his ways. She did not even stop to think that anything he had done was wrong. He was the man she loved. The man she was going to marry. The man whose baby she thought she might be expecting. The man with so many bloody victims. The man who did not care about anything other than her. She remembered how, just a few days earlier, Lewis had given her a beautiful sapphire ring to celebrate their engagement.

'There you go sugar. Now we are one.'

It was the first time Eileen had ever been given anything in the name of love. She looked at the well-crafted ring and ran her finger tips across the smooth stone. She did not ask where he got it from.

She already knew. But she did not care. She did not care that he had taken it from the corpse of one of his victims. She had been a woman very much like Shirley Denogean. Same sort of age. Same sort of dress. In fact they had robbed and killed her after kidnapping her at the Puente Hills Mall as well. That Mall was supposed to be the prime example of safe shopping for a safe society. John Lewis, Robbin Machuca, Eileen Huber and Vincent Hubbard had made sure that all those illusions had been well and truly shattered.

'I said go ahead and kill me now!'

Shirley Denogean shouted the last word at the top of her voice and smashed her fist down on Lewis' neck and tried to grab the gun out of his lap.

For a few wild moments, he lost control of the car and it skidded across two lanes of the Pomona Freeway. Luckily there was no traffic nearby. Shirley must have wished there had been. Then, at least she might have stood a chance of surviving this living nightmare.

Lewis was furious. His empty emotionless behaviour had been replaced by a fit of temper that was truly terrifying.

He swung his fist across Shirley's face.

'Shut up you fucking bitch.'

The atmosphere inside the Mercedes was now unbelievable. But Shirley was not sobbing. She was angry. Angrier than she had ever been before in her entire life. She was not going to die easily. If they wanted to kill her they had better get a move on because she was going to fight them all the way. Behind the Mercedes, Robbin was apprehensive. She did not care about that woman. But she did worry about her brother and Eileen. They had almost got themselves killed a few seconds earlier. They had to get rid of that piece of trash. Robbin considered Shirley to be just another victim — nothing more or less. She had no feelings about her. But then people she had been much closer to during her own painful life had not cared about her. She thought about her step-father. The so-called, loving father figure who crept into her bed at nights and raped her. She thought about her mother. The one person in the world who should have loved and protected her. Instead, she allowed that animal to carry on his attacks unhindered. Never once did she step in and stop those brutal sex attacks. Not once.

Robbin didn't care about Shirley Denogean. Why should she? Human decency had long ago ceased to exist in her life.

'Go on. Go ahead and kill me.'

Lewis couldn't stand this woman a moment longer. Why didn't she just shut up? Why was she making it all so fucking painful? Shirley knew this was her only opportunity. She had to harass and hinder them as much as possible. Then she might stand a chance. Her instincts would not allow her to give up the fight. She wanted to live.

But all she was actually doing was forcing Lewis

and Eileen to face a situation they had already dealt with on at least three previous occasions. They saw themselves as latter day Bonny and Clydes. Rightfully taking what they felt was theirs. Shirley was making a nuisance of herself. Her time had come. Lewis pulled the Mercedes over onto the hard shoulder of the freeway. Just a few yards behind, Robbin came to a halt in Eileen's Mercury.

'I am not getting out. You'll have to kill me first.'

Shirley just would not give in. She knew they would never shoot her there in front of all those passing motorists. If she refused to budge maybe, just maybe, she still stood a chance.

But Lewis was not going to let Shirley stand in his way. He lent into the back of the car and pulled the grandmother out of the seat of her own Mercedes. This was just another one to Lewis. Another face. Another day. Another victim. When Shirley Denogean looked into Lewis' eyes at that moment she knew he did not care. She knew that her death sentence was already confirmed.

At gunpoint, he made her walk along the side of the freeway towards an embankment. Just behind, Eileen and Robbin followed. They knew what was about to happen. They had seen it all before. But Robbin did not flinch when Eileen stopped walking and hung back so as not to see what was about to happen.

'Lie down.'

Shirley did not flinch despite the order from Lewis.

'I said fucking lie down — bitch.'

Shirley Denogean was not about to lose her dignity after all this time. She turned and looked into Lewis' eyes. He tried to avert her gaze. He felt uncomfortable. He hated the way she was looking at him. He felt challenged. But he also felt uneasy. She would not lie down and let him shoot her in the back. She was still looking straight at him. He couldn't handle it. This was not the way it was with the others. He could not shoot into her face and look at those eyes staring at him.

He aimed the revolver at her stomach and pulled the trigger. Whether he hoped to kill her or just injure her we will never know. Shirley fell to the ground instantly. She clutched her stomach but she was still very much alive. Lewis turned and walked away. He could not stand to look at her a moment longer. He did not care if she lived or died but he could not bear to see those eyes again.

'Bastard. You bastard.'

Shirley wanted him to know. She wanted him to realise what he had actually just done. Lewis could not stand the noise of her screaming.

He turned around, walked back towards her and lifted his gun. This time he pulled the trigger again and again and again. Each time a shot rang out he saw her body jerk with the force of the bullet as it entered.

The first shot entered her shoulder and split open a gaping wound. Bits of flesh flew upwards.

The next bullet ripped into the side of her body. But still Shirley fought back.

'Bastard. Bastard. Bastard.'

'Why don't you shut the fuck up bitch?'

Lewis aimed at the head this time. That shut her yapping. He hated the noise. He hated the screaming. It reminded him of reform school when the kids yelled so loudly in the playground before they beat him up. But worst of all, it reminded him of his perverted stepfather and how he would shout at him in fury before forcing him onto the bed.

'SHUT UP! SHUT UP! SHUT UP! SHUT UP!'

With each word he fired again and again. John Lewis had to get all those dreadful memories out of his mind for ever.

Peppering a twitching, innocent human being was a therapeutic way of cleansing his soul. When it was all over he looked up and saw his half sister Robbin looking down at him. She smiled. She approved. They had nothing to lose.

Lewis, Machuca, Hubbard and Huber were arrested in September 1991 after detectives identified them from security photographs taken by one of the cash dispenser machines. An alert shop keeper also took the registration number of Eileen's Mercury when they tried to use some of their stolen credit cards in a clothes store.

All four were accused of at least four other similar random killings that terrorised the residents of the San Gabriel Valley in August 1991.

10

The Blood-Sucking She-Devils

The sound of cricket-song mingled with the gentle lapping of the river. Every now and again passing cars lit up the roadside as they weaved their way home. The lights from nearby houses went out as their owners retired to bed.

Suddenly, a metallic green saloon span out of the darkness and screeched to a halt in the dusty car park of the Lew-Mors nightclub. The ten-year-old Holden Commodore had definitely seen better days. An entirely functional car, it was often described as the Vauxhall Viva of Australia. Its shape was designed with common sense — and absolutely no style — in mind.

But that didn't worry Bobby. She was a tough, brutal, masculine woman. More concerned with sex, drink and drugs than the remotest thoughts of family responsibilities or any of the standard domestic concerns.

She stumbled into the Lew-Mors with three girlfriends. She was already drunk from having consumed at least ten beers in a tiny bar just half a mile away. As she entered the club, she passed through the tatty lobby and caught a glimpse of herself in a mirror and grimaced. She hated mirrors. They were a sad reflection of her inner self. Then she felt a strange pain in her head. And it wasn't caused by the loud music blaring out from the dance floor.

This was a pain from within. Bobby was fighting something — but she did not know what.

Once inside the club, Bobby's notoriously promiscuous temperament took over. She had spotted an attractive woman sitting with a friend in a corner of the club traditionally reserved for those seeking a new partner.

The girl was in her early twenties and had medium length brown hair. It was difficult to tell what her figure was like but her bizarre outfit was arousing a lot of attention, which was precisely what was intended. She wore a long black coat, stockings, high heeled shoes and a white tuxedo-style shirt with a black bow tie. She seemed almost satanic. That really appealed to Bobby.

Their eyes met instantly. They each knew what the other was thinking. Bobby's pals were at the bar buying drinks. She loved to tease and flirt first — it was always much more fun. As her friends brought over the beers, Bobby turned her back to the girl in the corner. Every now and again she would sneak a glimpse of her.

The three friends supped greedily at their drinks. But Bobby's mind was on that girl, her vivid imagination working overtime. She was seeing her partly clothed on a bed. Vulnerable, excited, desperate. She wanted her. She would have her.

Bobby's sexual drive knew few boundaries. After all, here she was preparing for her next conquest, just a few hours after making brutal love to the girl she lived with. They had both arrived home early from college and neither of their two other flatmates were around. Bobby had grabbed her from behind in the kitchen and smothered her neck in kisses. At first her friend resisted, but Bobby was forceful and strong. Soon she was holding her down as she ground into her body. It was all over in minutes but that sexual drive was satisfied — at least for a while.

Back in the club, one of Bobby's friends was telling a crude joke. But they were all well aware that Bobby wasn't listening.

'She's all yours. Stop fantasising. Just get over there and pull her.'

This was a Friday night in Brisbane, Australia. The whole town was out to enjoy the weekend. In these sunny climes, it was an excuse to commit a multitude of sins.

That was all the prompting Bobby needed. She

could already feel her heart beat faster with excitement. A sexual thrill was rushing through her body, even though she hadn't spoken to the girl yet.

With black trousers and black t-shirt, hobnail boots and an ever-present pair of wire rimmed sunglasses, Bobby hardly exuded glamour. But, in a club like the Lew-Mors, no one exactly dressed up for dinner.

The place was full of hard cases all hoping to find a passion partner to share their bodies with. The dance floor was poorly lit. Soul music throbbed out of the loud speakers as couples gyrated together.

Bobby turned to face her admirer once more and their eyes met again. This time she did not hesitate. As she strode confidently over to the table, the girl squirmed expectantly in her seat. Lisa knew she was about to be swept off her feet.

The two talked a while. But deep, meaningful conversation was not exactly high on their list of priorities. They both knew what the other wanted.

That night was Friday the thirteenth of October, 1989.

Unlucky for some …

Lisa Ptaschinski curled up beside her sleeping lover. They had met just a few hours earlier, but she felt as if they had known each other for most of their life. On both her wrists were two tiny fresh scabs. Lisa looked at them and once more felt a rush to her brain as she remembered the sexual thrill she had experienced less than an hour before.

Within seconds of getting back to the

apartment, these two strangers were exploring every inch of each other's bodies. After their first climax, both wanted more, not less.

It was then that Lisa discovered her partner liked to play a game that even she had never tried before. As the two lovers lay back to recover from that first crescendo, they started to talk about blood. The taste of it. The smell of it. Even the colour of it. The more they talked about blood, the more excited Bobby became.

She was disarmingly frank: 'I think I'm a vampire. I can't resist blood. Its taste. Even its texture. Something inside me craves for it.'

For a moment Lisa stopped and stared at Bobby. Then she felt really good. Her brand new lover was already revealing her innermost thoughts to her. She wanted to please Bobby in every way.

Then, without a word, Lisa got up out of bed. A look of disappointment came over her lover's face. She presumed that she was getting up to go. But within moments Lisa had returned. Armed with a pointed kitchen knife she said simply, 'Surprise ...'

The tiny droplets of blood had to be literally coaxed out of Lisa's veins at first. But as her lover sucked harder, she felt a slight, but pleasurable pain from her wrist. Then the sucking got even stronger and she could feel the excitement building up inside. As a gesture of her passion, Lisa then stabbed gently at the vein on her other wrist and watched as her lover's face looked up at her, a tiny drip of blood dribbling down the side of the mouth as it curled into a smile of satisfaction, just like a cat who's got the cream.

Every now and again, Bobby kissed the tender flesh near Lisa's wrist, as if to assure her that she wasn't just into blood. But it was purely a token gesture for, within seconds, she would return to her favoured feast. She was captivated by Lisa's flawless complexion. Her skin really was as perfect as it looked. And it felt as smooth as syrup.

Lisa's legs were ever so slightly parted as Bobby sucked deeper and deeper into her. She could feel her breath speeding up. This was as exciting as those first days of sexual experimentation she had carried out at her convent school in Sydney. Lisa loved to feel she could constantly supply pleasure. It was almost more important to her than receiving satisfaction.

Now Bobby was gently moaning to herself — the excitement carrying a throaty noise that she emitted from within. It was a strange noise — sometimes high pitched, sometimes deep. A struggling noise.

Now the groans of pleasure were becoming louder as Lisa and Bobby moaned in unison. Bobby's sounds were sheer enjoyment. Lisa's were an extraordinary combination of pain and pleasure. The pain from the sucking, the pleasure came from giving.

As the pewter light of dawn shone through the opened window, the lovers continued, oblivious to the outside world. Locked in a dangerous, erotic world from which neither wanted to escape.

The Observer looked in at the scene. One lover lay on her back with her wrists flat on the bed as her partner feasted on the blood.

Neither of them noticed that a third party had entered the room. They were so wrapped up in the passion and the pain that they were oblivious to their surroundings.

'This is sick,' muttered the Observer to herself, disgusted by the scene before her. Appalled. Yet fascinated. So she stayed in the room as the two lovers writhed, explored ... and drank.

She wanted to stop them but something prevented her. Something made her stay there and witness this degradation. But she did not know what. And she did not know why ...

Next morning, the two lovers held hands tightly at every available opportunity. With each squeezing motion, Lisa felt a slight twinge of pain in the scabs on her wrists. But it was a bearable pain. A sacrifice worth making for the one she adored.

As Bobby made breakfast, eight-year-old Tracey Wigginton appeared. She was a regular visitor to the flat. A child whose very presence was difficult to ever explain.

'What are you doing?' she asked in the blunt manner that only a child can get away with. 'Are you in love?'

Bobby looked embarrassed. After all, how could she explain her actions to an eight-year-old? Love is something that children have an instinct for — and they are usually right.

Little Tracey was desperate for love. She was brought up by her grandparents. But actually they were not really her mother's parents. To make matters worse, her step-grandfather had abused her. Verbally by day and sexually by night. She had never forgotten how he used to get in her bed. Her life was messed up and she longed for security. That's why she often came into Bobby's life.

She missed out on real, normal emotions and could only relate to the harsh reality of a miserable, tortured environment. Now she was trying to make up for lost time … She soon disappeared from the apartment as quickly as she had arrived …

In less than twenty-four hours, Bobby and Lisa became close — close enough that Bobby decided to introduce Lisa to her great friends Tracey Waugh and Kim Jervis. Lisa was reluctant at first. After all, why should Bobby want her to meet two of her other women friends? They were probably lovers as well. She already felt pangs of jealousy. But Bobby was very forceful about it. 'You'll love them. We can all have a good time together.'

Lisa knew there was no way out — and maybe Bobby was right. When she wanted her own way, she usually got it.

As it happened, the foursome got on famously.

Lisa's fears were unfounded. She started to not even care if Bobby had slept with any of them.

Tracey was twenty-four, an unemployed secretary. Dressed in a more feminine sort of way than her friends she seemed altogether a softer sort of character. Kim, the same age, was the only member of the group with a full-time job — as a photo processor. An attention-grabbing kind of girl, she lapped up every word uttered by Bobby. Appreciative of the friendship and all that it could lead to.

As they all drank their ice-cool beer and swapped tales of life, Lisa happily acknowledged to herself that she was being swept up by Bobby and her friends. She'd always wanted a close circle of companions. Now she had found one.

Then Kim cracked a joke about blood. The table went silent. Bobby breathed — sharply. If they had been in a restaurant or bar, perhaps the atmosphere would have swept the conversation forward and everyone would have simply ignored the remark. But this scene was being played out in Kim's spotless suburban apartment in the Clayfield area of Brisbane. The atmosphere already bordered on the intimate. Now there was a chance to take it a stage further.

Bobby dimmed the lights and returned to the table where they were all sitting. She obviously had something important to contribute. Turning to her self-appointed protégé, Kim, she said coolly, 'I want to scare you.'

The other three sat in total silence.

Bobby removed her sunglasses and stared straight into their eyes, each in turn.

'She wanted to use her mind to make us compatible,' explained Kim later. Quite simply, Bobby wanted to mind-control her friends. She wanted to have the power over them that she lusted for constantly.

But first, she wanted to make Kim her 'destroyer'. That role meant Kim would become her disciple. Her messenger of all things.

The atmosphere was tightening by the second. Only Tracey remained somewhat sceptical but, as she was later to recall, 'I was powerless to do anything. She had us in the palm of her hand.'

Bobby was getting tough. 'I have satanic powers and you will all become my disciples in time.'

Lisa was fascinated. This sort of experience was what she had been looking for all her life. She was vulnerable. She desperately needed to be led — and Bobby was providing that lead.

Bobby got up from the table and picked a thick photo album out of a drawer in a nearby cupboard. She then spread the pictures across the table — about fifteen in all. They were all shots of headstones from nearby Harrisville Cemetery.

Bobby was convinced that each of the featured graves belonged to the devil. She talked of how they would come out at night and drive people to commit evil crimes.

'This is the way of the devil. You must realise

this,' she said, her strange voice veering from low, deep tones to a high, almost falsetto, shrill.

At no stage did any of the women even so much as question her claims — only Tracey had any doubts and she knew that now was not the time to air them.

It was only later that Tracey realised the significance of the fact that all the curtains in the apartment were closed, even though it was still daylight outside. The only explanation at the time was that Bobby was sensitive to sunlight. They had always been aware that she hated to go out in the day.

But Bobby was now concerned with bringing the conversation around to vampires.

'They do exist. I know. I am one,' she insisted. 'I need blood. I must have it.'

The women watched in silence as Bobby went up to the fridge and took out a white butcher's plastic bag filled with blood. She devoured the entire contents carelessly, or perhaps thirstily, spilling drops on her T-shirt.

At that moment Tracey spotted the tiny scabs on Lisa's wrists and smiled a knowing smile. They were all becoming Bobby's disciples.

'I hunger for blood all the time. I need it in me,' continued Bobby. No one sitting there was in the slightest bit surprised.

Bobby openly revealed she had feasted on the blood of virtually every type of livestock animal. She was a regular at a handful of butchers' shops in the area near her home. They learned not to raise an eyebrow at her bizarre requests for vast quantities of pig's blood. It had become a necessity as well as an obsession. Each day, she said, she had to drink blood.

But animal blood did not really satisfy the appetite within her.

There was another, deeper need. And she wanted to feed it, to nurture it until it consumed her.

Every other person at that table had, at one time or other, given in to Bobby's demands. They all had the tell-tale scabs on their wrists.

Bobby wanted more than just an ounce or two of blood this time. She wanted pints of the stuff. Human blood. And it had to be fresh because 'that way it is cleaner and smoother and tastier.'

She added chillingly, 'By the time our man hits the ground his throat will be cut and he'll be dead.'

Then she put a proposition to her friends. 'Help me find a victim.'

Ted Baldock was in a pretty good mood. It was Friday afternoon and soon he would be finished with work for the weekend. A weekend that would no doubt include the two extremes of his life as a father-of-five — drunkenness and domesticity.

The weather was swelteringly hot. About ninety-five degrees in the shade. Brisbane in October was like a July day in New York. Sweat dripped off his lean shoulders.

For Ted it was harder than most. No air-conditioned office for him to sit back in. His workplace was the roads of the city and his 'typewriter' was a pneumatic drill that throbbed and hammered into the sun-baked tarmac.

Ted had struggled hard for nearly thirty years to support his huge family. He and wife Elaine had found it pretty difficult at times. But they had survived all the ups and downs that married life could throw at them. Ted had a thick skin that proved ideal for a lifelong marriage. Now, at forty-seven, he was starting to look forward to retirement, a pension and blissful relaxation after years of providing. Maybe a bit of fishing, probably a fair deal of boozing. But no pressures. No demands.

His body ached with exhaustion from the hard week he had endured. Ted was not your macho-muscle man like many of his colleagues on the road repair squad for Brisbane City Council. He was a modest sort of fellow. Not prone to even taking his shirt off in public — let alone flaunting his biceps. Elaine and many of his friends at home in the West End district of Brisbane were always telling Ted not to overdo it.

As he jerked the drill into place for the last time on the roadside, his thoughts were rapidly wandering to the weekend. If he'd known what lay ahead, he'd have stopped thinking there and then …

The Holden Commodore came to a halt outside Lisa's home in Leichardt. She heard her lover sound the horn twice. As the pretty, brown haired girl looked out of the window of the tiny box-built house, their eyes locked. It was almost the same feeling as that first time they had met and seduced each other just seven days earlier.

Landlady Wendy Sugden was curious. She felt a great deal of responsibility for Lisa since the day, just five weeks earlier, they had met at Ipswich General Hospital. Lisa was a patient, and Wendy, her nurse, had taken her under her wing. They struck up a real friendship.

Lisa looked upon Wendy as a mother figure. Always there when she was needed. Providing a vital support to lean on. Wendy and her husband Wayne had an ordinary little house, but it was clean and tidy and the nearest thing to home that Lisa had ever known. When she told Wendy about Bobby, the nurse frowned. She sounded like trouble but then Lisa was always going to be a problem person.

As Lisa skipped out of the front door to her waiting admirer, she thought back to that first night of outrageous passion. Then, as if to reassure herself, she scratched the top of the tiny scab on her left wrist — just to make sure that every moment of lust they shared had actually happened.

The two lovers kissed deeply within moments of Lisa getting in the car. Lisa could feel the body heat oozing off her partner. If it hadn't still been daylight they might have made love there and then.

Wendy watched everything from a ground floor window, saddened by the inevitability that it would all end in tears ... or worse. She'd seen it all before. Lisa's life revolved around disastrous relationships.

Lisa looked at her lover for a moment as they untangled themselves. A new, darker, midnight black hairstyle made her features far more severe than when they last met. Bobby was looking more and more like the vampire she had convinced herself she was.

Lisa did not notice the bulge in Bobby's black jacket pocket. She could only think forward to another night of sex. She knew there was going to be a real 'treat' in store for Bobby this time.

It was a thirty minute drive to the other girls' homes. During that time, Bobby kept saying how hungry she was. How she was looking forward to feasting. Her appetite for blood had definitely increased.

Her thirst would soon be quenched.

But first, they had to pick up Kim and Tracey from their apartments in Clayfield.

Kim and Tracey jumped into the car, chatting rapidly, eager expectation etched on their faces. Once again, Lisa failed to notice another bulge — this time in Kim's pocket.

If she had looked inside that pocket, she would have seen a ninja butterfly pocket knife with a 10cm blade. Kim had bought it in the nearby Fortitude Valley army disposal shop after they'd discussed their plans ...

Ted Baldock was back at the council changing rooms stripping off his filthy work clothes before showering in preparation for a Friday night on the town. Like millions of manual workers the world over, Ted took a great pride in dressing up whenever he went out. It was as if he longed for the clean-cut life of an office worker. Wearing a smart pair of slacks and a newly starched shirt was a real pleasure.

For him, the grass was always greener on the other side. There were many things he longed for in life.

As he washed himself under a piping hot cascade of water, he felt the energy returning to those tired bones. Ted was looking forward with relish to the first glass of beer of the day. He felt he deserved to treat himself.

For the previous six Fridays, Ted, sometimes with Elaine in tow, had become a regular of the Caledonian Club at Kangaroo Point. It was a rough and ready joint but Ted liked the atmosphere and no one stopped you drinking however much you wanted. You could sup to your heart's content, and no one gave a damn. So long as you didn't puke on the floor, that is.

He'd discovered the place after being taken there by a workmate. It was a great escape from the tedium of a week spent working on the roads and watching mindless TV at his West End home.

As he strolled the short distance from the council changing rooms to the Caledonian, he could literally smell the beer in his nostrils. It was a good feeling. He was going to have a great time tonight. He could feel it in his blood.

The girls had all agreed that the Lew-Mors was the perfect place to start their night out, to savour the anticipation. But Bobby was anxious now. Counting the minutes. It had to be midnight before they could strike. It was no use before then. It had to be just like the Dracula books she used to read so avidly when she was at school.

Instead of beers and spirits, the four friends ordered champagne. This evening was special. Soon they would have something extraordinary to celebrate.

The club manageress was astounded. 'They were buzzing with excitement,' she said when she looked back on that fateful night. And some of the regulars thought the weird foursome were planning an orgy.

As they sat at a table just by the DJ's booth, the girls drank a toast … to blood. The blood of a human who still had no idea he was to become their victim.

Ted had spent hours indulging in his favourite game, darts. After a few beers, he was taking on everyone and losing. But no one minded, Ted was a good loser. Always good for a laugh.

He ended the evening holding up the bar. Or perhaps the bar was holding up him. Either way the two inanimate objects were getting along just fine. This sort of vast beer consumption was nothing new for Ted and the barmen were happy to keep on feeding him alcohol because he wasn't making a pest of himself.

Every now and again he would talk to an acquaintance about the meaning of life. But it would only be a passing gesture — nothing of a seriously friendly nature. No one in the bar that evening was a great friend of Ted Baldock.

It was getting towards midnight and that meant it was time for all the Teds of Brisbane to get on their merry way home. As last orders were called, he persuaded a barman to give him one last refill. He downed it quickly, stumbled out into the balmy night, and concentrated, in vain, on finding his way home.

He knew that Elaine — while a loving, caring and patient wife — would not tolerate his non-appearance, whatever the excuse.

Across town, Bobby, Lisa, Kim and Tracey were finishing off their second bottle of bubbly.

'What are you celebrating? Love and marriage?' asked one hostess.

The four giggled in expectation. Bobby admired the girl's shapely legs.

'Wouldn't you like to know, sweetheart,' she cooed seductively.

Lisa felt a twinge of jealousy. Bobby had the sort of eyes that probed everywhere. Every time a pretty girl passed by, she could sense Bobby's eyes upon their body, sizing up the sex content. She

consoled herself by remembering she was hers —
even if Bobby did fantasise about the size of the
waitress' breasts.

The champagne was now really having an effect
and all four felt the headiness unique to France's
favourite drink. They felt sensuous, carefree, daring.
There was a buzz in the air. Bobby kept talking
about her hunger. Her appetite. Her obsession.
Blood.

She was the one person at that table who really
knew what lay ahead …

Outside the Lew-Mors, the hunt was about to begin.
It was dead on midnight. Everything was perfect.
Bobby had the expectant look of someone about to
win a huge prize.

'I'll drive. Then you can pick one,' said Lisa as
they got into Bobby's car. At first, Bobby was
reluctant to allow Lisa to drive. She was the 'man' in
their relationship and it was her car. But then she
saw the sense in what Lisa was saying. No one else
could choose the victim except Bobby.

To begin with, they drove at a steady 30 mph
towards the Botanic Gardens district of the city. It
was a lively night-time area — perfect for what they
had in mind. For ten minutes they drove around the
streets hovering outside the nightclubs and pubs, but
there was no suitable prey.

Then they headed for the New Farm Park area
and they soon spotted a lonely figure staggering in a
zig-zag along the pavement. The Commodore

slowed down. This was what they were looking for.

The man turned and faced straight into the car's headlights. He looked perfect.

But then another man appeared from an alleyway. Two was too many. Too difficult to handle. They had to be patient.

They drove on, disappointed.

Bobby did not feel like being patient. She was hungry. She couldn't wait. It was past midnight. Feeding time.

Then they decided to head for Kangaroo Point. A last resort. There had to be someone around.

The night sounded empty and strangely quiet. It was almost as if a massive storm had passed and left in its wake an eerie, dead calm. A thin, motionless fog hung near the water's edge, catching the silver light of the moon.

Sprawled face down on the pavement lay Ted Baldock. He wasn't actually out cold. But he was definitely suffering. He blinked and waited in the hope that things would come back into focus. He inhaled deep breaths of air to try to compose himself. He had to make it home to Elaine and the children.

Gradually his vision began to clear and he hauled himself up from the ground grasping on to a lamp-post for support. As he clambered to his feet, the headlights of an approaching car shone fiercely in his eyes.

All he could see was a blur of light. He wasn't

even sure if it was moving at first. It was only when the vehicle got closer that he could make out a car. For a moment, Ted forgot where he was or how he had got there. He tried to concentrate and was pleasantly surprised. It wasn't that hard after all. That brief 'rest' on the sidewalk had definitely helped recover his senses.

The car was getting closer. Ted was trying to get his mind around what all this meant. Maybe he could thumb a lift or maybe it was a taxi. He felt in his pockets. He had some money. He tried to flag it down.

In the pitch black, Ted couldn't begin to even guess the size and shape of the occupants — it was all too much for his addled brain to cope with. But being a friendly drunk leaning against a lamp-post, he could not imagine their intentions were anything other than honourable.

'You want a ride?' a woman's voice beckoned. Kim and Bobby had got out of the car. They felt they should guide him to the vehicle.

Ted did not hesitate.

He hauled himself off the lamp-post and headed, unsteadily, in the direction of the car. One step at a time at first. Then, as his confidence grew, he began to walk more steadily. The couple opened the passenger door and another female voice beckoned.

'Come on in.'

Then one of them helped Ted in. He found himself hemmed between two attractive looking long-

haired women in their early twenties — and he wasn't
complaining. The whole thing seemed so unreal.

He could only just make out the hair of one
woman in front and the short back and sides of the
female driver.

Ted was sobering up now. These girls were out
for some fun. He couldn't believe his luck. They
stroked his body through his clothes, kissed his ear
and nibbled his neck. He felt himself harden at the
prospect of all these girls. Who knows? Maybe he'd
get a ride home as part of the bargain.

'You want to have some real fun?' asked one
girl. Ted didn't even need to bother replying. There
was only one real answer. He had money. But he
wasn't even sure if they wanted it. They just seemed
to want him.

The car stopped just near the prestigious South
Brisbane Yacht Club. But it was way past those
yachtsmen's bedtimes and the place was silent and
locked up for the night.

Midnight had come and gone and Bobby was
hungry. Very hungry.

She told a dazed Ted to go down to the river's
edge with her to sort out the money and then the
girls would join him. This really was turning out to
be Ted's lucky night.

It was the first time he had tried to walk since
struggling to the car just a few minutes earlier. Yet,
now he had a fresh motive and, although still very
drunk, he had purpose in his walk. He knew where
he was going and he thought he knew precisely

what he was about to get from these girls.

As Ted approached the river's edge, Bobby went back to the car. What little light there was disappeared from view. There had been a streetlight some half a mile away but now it was gone.

Splinters of wood that had been blown off the trees by recent gales crackled beneath his feet.

Back in the Holden Commodore, Kim and Tracey were scared.

'Let's just leave him there,' they both pleaded. But Lisa and Bobby had other plans.

Just moments before, they had all watched the pathetic figure of Ted walking down to the riverside to prepare for his night of passion. But they all knew that he was there only to provide the thrills for them.

Bobby was angry with Kim and Tracey. After all, they had all agreed on this 'celebration'. Now there was a breakdown of discipline in the ranks. But the two mutineers refused to budge.

In an act of defiance Kim flung her knife on to the front arm rest of the car. Bobby scowled at her, then grabbed it and stormed off.

On the riverbank, Ted stripped off completely. Despite all the drink he had consumed he had the good sense to put his wallet and keys in one of his shoes. The last thing he wanted was to lose anything valuable.

Then he sat — a slightly ludicrous figure — naked on the bank and waited for his women to appear.

It was pitch black and the only sound was the

river lapping gently on the bank. Every now and again there would be a plop in the water as an insect hit the surface.

A voice then told Ted to move to a clearer strip of river bank just a few yards upstream. It was Bobby's voice — but it had become high pitched and difficult to distinguish. Also, it was said with such command that anyone would have felt obliged to obey it.

Ted turned to see who it was but there was no one there. He just presumed that the order was a guarantee of what was to come. He readily obeyed — convinced that his happy moment was fast approaching.

As he walked the short distance, he spotted what he thought was his credit card. In the poor light, Ted did not even check to see if it was actually his.

Instead, he just dropped it into one of his shoes for safe-keeping. He neatly laid out his clothes in a pile. It seemed as sensible a place as any to put your valuables when you are about to indulge in some casual sex with girls you have never met before.

'He's going to be too strong for just me.' Bobby turned to Lisa. 'You've got to come.'

Lisa hesitated for a moment and then looked into those piercing eyes and felt obliged to aid her lover. She knew exactly what was intended. She had encouraged it because she wanted Bobby to be satisfied. She could not retreat now. They were lovers and you always do whatever your lover wants.

The two girls in the back looked stunned, but they kept their thoughts to themselves. They were now shivering with fright, holding each other other for comfort, desperate to escape from this nightmare and return to reality.

Bobby grasped Lisa's hand. That slight pain from the scab on her vein returned as if to remind her of what was to come. They walked gingerly around the back of the yacht club to where Ted was waiting patiently.

They were systematically holding their breath and then releasing short bursts of air, so as not to make much noise. Lisa's hand was hot and clammy. Bobby's was cool, almost ice cool, considering the heat of the night. They both realised one thing — the element of surprise was essential ...

Ted was getting irritated. He wanted sex and it was not forthcoming. He was fed up with sitting on that riverbank. Although his vision was adapting well to the poor light, he failed to see the two figures approaching him from behind.

Bobby and Lisa could now clearly see Ted's back in the moonlight. He had that slightly loose skin that many men get as they approach their fifties. He was crouching, awkwardly swinging from side to side. Occasionally, Ted would shake his head to force himself awake after nodding off to sleep.

Each time he fell into a slumber, he would begin to dream vivid visions — only to snap himself awake. He was waiting for an orgy to begin and those dreams were becoming so daunting.

Bobby had a shiny object in each hand and Lisa could see in her eyes that same look that came over her whenever they were about to make love.

They stopped some yards short of Ted and quietly removed their clothes. They wanted to guarantee that Ted would not struggle until they were ready to feast. The sight of two lithe, female bodies in the dark would leave him in no doubt of their intent.

Ted shifted his position slightly as the two lovers approached. He looked behind and could just make out their naked bodies. He glanced at them before looking out to the river once more. He could not believe his luck — two nubile, young girls. Wait till he told his mates at work about this. He was happy to wait for them to come to him — after all he was going to pay. If he had stared a little harder he would have seen, rather than felt, the first frenzy of knife stabs that were soon to rain down on him from Bobby's hands.

Bobby was shaking with need. She needed blood. Here she was, about to kill as she stood in the dark on the river bank. Something inside was urging her to murder an innocent man.

She was going to kill. There was nothing she could do to stop it. The more she thought of her own cruel upbringing, the more she failed to shame herself about committing murder. She could not control her hunger.

Many people thought that murder was a sin. Bobby reckoned she knew otherwise. Some were born with a taste for blood. Others had it instilled in them. Bobby always claimed she drank the blood of live goats when she ran away from her cruel 'grandparents' at the age of just 15.

But God had made each man as he was and Bobby had been chosen to kill. It was all part of the masterplan. In Bobby's eyes, the only sin was to kill when your lover did not approve of the victim. But they had all chosen this victim together. They all knew what Bobby wanted. That gave her the licence to kill …

Standing there, watching by the river's edge was the Observer. She was shocked. How could Bobby kill? She should be ashamed by her terrible actions. Surely it was not too late to stop? But the beast within Bobby would always ignore the truth. And the Observer knew that, really. She was powerless to stop the onslaught. It was out of her control.

As Bobby got closer, the dead calm returned. Like beasts prowling in the night, they slowed down as they approached their victim. Then they paused momentarily, waiting for the perfect moment.

The Observer was now pleading, begging Bobby to stop. Stop now.

Bobby knew what she was being told. She knew that what she was doing was wrong. But the urge from within was still too strong to resist.

'Stop. Stop. Stop,' the Observer screamed. 'This

is crazy. Insane. Get a hold of yourself ...' But the words were soon lost in the wind. Never to return.

Bobby let out one long pent-up breath. Her family had never really taught her that killing was wrong. But then they were not a proper family. They had never drawn the moral lines that every child so desperately needs. Instead, she had been beaten and abused whenever she committed a wrong-doing. No one ever explained why. Often Bobby would be locked in her room as a child and visited by her grandfather when he wanted to hurt her or have sex with her — or worse.

On other occasions, Bobby's family could look straight through her, as if she didn't even exist. They never provided any warmth, comfort or security. Instead, she was told how bad she was. How the very mention of her name would make them feel sick. How she was a lazy, no-good, evil little brat.

They would take out the belt and thrash her. Now, she wanted to show them, show them all just how evil she really was.

But Bobby was sure her horrible family would understand why she could not control herself on this night. They might not forgive her, but they would inspire her to commit the deed. Bobby reckoned she knew where all those relatives would end up — and it certainly was not heaven. Then the girls pounced.

Ted buckled and thrashed as he fell onto his back but he couldn't shake off the assault. He no longer had the strength. He gurgled and spluttered as his mouth filled with blood and rapidly his convulsions became less violent before fading altogether.

Fifteen times Bobby plunged her two knives into Ted's shoulders. A soft ripping sound came with each stab. One after the other they rained in on him, the blood seeping out of each wound. Bobby was now pomelling the knives, rather than grinding them, into his body. It was the same action as if she were thumping her fists on a table. She could not stop. Ted lay motionless on his back, but it didn't stop Bobby. She attacked his neck and chest just to make doubly sure there was no more life left in the mutilated corpse.

In a way this part of the attack was even more frenzied. Ted could not fight back and that invited a more ferocious response.

All the time she was stabbing with the knife she thought of her family. Of how she had begged them for love. But none of them would forgive her for inflicting herself upon them.

Ted was now a tangled mound of a body, crumpled on the grassy embankment. With the ninja knife, Bobby coldly and calmly slit Ted's throat from ear to ear. Lisa watched in fascination. She was so excited by the sight of her lover's naked body. She knew all about her urges and she wanted to see those cravings satisfied.

Bobby crouched over the body and began to lick and drink the blood that poured from the victim's throat. More memories came flooding back.

Bobby recalled how she had discovered her grandmother was not her real blood relative. How she was told her mother had abandoned her. None of her seven brothers and sisters were related to her. Life had been one long betrayal.

No one could be trusted.

She swirled her tongue around the inside of the gaping wound, trying to devour every last morsel. But there was more than enough there.

She pushed the severed head further back to expose the throat wound even further — giving her more access to the blood. Now she was devouring the flesh like a shark in a feeding frenzy. The skin ripped open like a PVC dustbin bag when it's been over-filled.

Bobby then turned to Lisa. She had a lip-curling smile that showed she had fed sufficiently — for the moment.

Businessman Scott Evans Gamble was sitting on the opposite side of the river bank when he heard the groans. A wry smile came to his face as they grew in sound to reach an ecstatic peak of what he presumed was sexual climax.

Lisa was now breathing in short and sharp gasps. She watched admiringly as her lover washed her body in the warm river water. Calmly, Bobby splashed water over her breasts and legs as if washing in a shower or bath.

She was only allowed one shallow bath a week

at home. This was fantastic. A whole river to lose oneself in. A torrent of never-ending water deep enough to swim in.

Once, at home, she was banned from eating at mealtime, because she urinated in the bath. Now she could do it to her heart's content and no one could stop her.

Soon the blood marks were washed away, but Bobby still had some other unfinished business to attend to. She strolled naked to the river bank where she picked up both the knives used in the killing and washed them lovingly in the river before carrying them back on to the river bank where the mutiliated torso lay twisted on its back by the muddy verge.

Both lovers stood there for a moment in the darkness, enveloped by the pungent aroma of blood. The smell was particularly strong when Bobby's breath wafted towards Lisa.

She could feel the globules of blood and flesh mixed together after becoming caught between her teeth. Using the tip of her tongue, Bobby tried to push them out from between the gaps.

Her first real taste of blood had come when she was swept up into a witches' coven near her home in Rock Hampton. She had been fascinated by the man and wife, whom the locals used to refer to as the witches.

They offered her a place to sleep. It was nicer than her foster parents' home. They often made sacrifices of animals like goats. They extended her education … in blood.

Bobby put on the jeans and T-shirt that were her regular 'uniform' around town. She was remarkably calm. Spent and satisfied like a lover who has just climaxed.

They walked back towards the car … hand in hand.

Watching them from nearby was the Observer. She was astounded. How could anyone do such a thing? A feeling of utter contempt and disgust came over her.

She kept repeating those eight words to herself. 'How could anyone do such a dreadful thing,' over and over. But she was powerless to act.

'I have just feasted. I have just feasted,' Bobby screamed again and again as they drove the 30 minute trip back to their homes.

The journey was truly bizarre. Tracey Waugh, close to tears, sat soberly in a corner of the back seat, terrified to speak. No one said much. All three women later recalled how they smelt the overwhelming aroma of the blood on Bobby's breath. It was pungent and nauseous. They said Bobby looked and behaved as if she had just enjoyed a three-course dinner.

Two boys were sitting in the back of a police squad car, shaking with fear. But this was not the fear of arrest. This was the shock of just having found the mutilated body of Ted Baldock.

Just a few yards away, behind the impressive facade of the South Brisbane Yacht Club, Detective Constable Danny Murdoch grimaced. He was a well-built cop with the likeable smile of a perennial optimist; but even his cheerful outlook on life was strained to breaking point by the sight that greeted him.

'The guy looks like he got the ultimate head job,' said Detective Constable Barry Deveney. Nobody laughed. It was 6.00am on Saturday October 21, and every detective called to the scene that day had been dragged in on a day off to join the murder inquiry.

The forensic team were already examining the area around the body for any minute clues. Murdoch leant down to examine Ted's clothes, which were still in a neat pile.

Policemen were cordoning off the area with white plastic tape. A small crowd had gathered just a few yards from the yacht club.

As the coroners' officers lifted the body into a zippered plastic corpse bag, some of the crowd grimaced. But they still continued to stare, fascinated by the macabre scene. They were detached from the emotion of losing a loved one. Just curious to take a look. To tell their friends they saw a body on the riverbank. It would be something to brag about when the conversation ran dry in the bars and pubs of Brisbane that night.

Murdoch picked up Ted's scruffy shoes and

heard the unmistakable, jangling noise of a set of keys. He reached inside to take them out and found a credit card. The name on it clearly read: Tracey Wigginton. That was Bobby's real name.

Detective Sergeant Glenn Burton, 40, was looking forward to a nice family Saturday at home. He had almost finished washing the car with his three children. And, unlike most husbands, he was more than happy to accompany his wife and kids to the supermarket.

Their home at Wynnum was a picturesque spot right on the bay. Beautiful views, beautiful weather. What more could a man ask for?

Glenn was putting the finishing touches to his car when he heard the phone. It was still early, so he knew it was unlikely to be family or friends. On occasions like this it was tempting not to answer or let one of the family say he was out. But Glenn Burton was not that kind of guy.

He was a straight man who knew that a policeman was never really off duty. He was just 'resting' between cases.

It was, therefore, hardly surprising when one of the kids said the call was for him. His assignment was to go and arrest the owner of that credit card.

Within minutes, Glenn was heading for Enoggera and the home of Tracey Wigginton. The police had a simple theory. Ted was murdered by a girlfriend and her other lover.

The clues were pretty well there for everyone to

see. The tyre marks from the car. The footsteps of two other people besides Ted. The ferocity of the stab wounds implied a woman had stood by and watched while her lover/husband carried out the killing.

As Glenn and five colleagues walked calmly up the stairs of the apartment block where Tracey Wigginton lived, it all seemed pretty clear cut.

Bobby was watching television. She had not slept well — mainly because Lisa did not stay the night with her. Bobby's three flat mates were sitting around drinking coffee, relaxing. It was a Saturday morning and they were all taking it easy.

There was a knock at the door. It was a firm, officious knock and Bobby knew instantly who it was. She went to answer it.

'Tracey Wigginton?' asked Glenn Burton.

'Bobby' had gone back into the subconscious of Tracey. She had taken on her real-life persona once more. There was no more eight-year-old Tracey to show innocence. Even the Observer was gone.

They had all returned into the mind of 23-year-old sheet metal college student Tracey Wigginton. The moment the police came calling, her four-way personality had dispersed. She could no longer hide behind those weird characters.

They were a part of her alter-ego. Not even the dominating force of Bobby could help. Tracey was going to have to cope with this living nightmare herself. There was no one else to turn to. Bobby never existed. Little Tracey never existed. The Observer was only her common sense telling her, warning her, what she was doing.

But this was reality. A reality that would cost Tracey Wigginton her liberty for the horrendous crime she had committed.

Bobby may have been in charge when those knives rained down on Ted Baldock's back. Bobby drank the blood and virtually severed the head to get more blood. Bobby seduced and lured Lisa Ptaschinski into joining those evil forces. But they'd all gone now, crawled back into the dark recesses of Tracey's troubled brain.

Tracey knew that as she opened that door, but she did not flinch. Her cold eyes stared confidently ahead as she faced Detective Sergeant Glenn Burton.

However, none of this was familiar territory for Glenn Burton. He still thought he was interviewing the estranged lover of Ted Baldock — not a multi-personality lesbian vampire with a lust for blood and murder.

The real Tracey Wigginton was a cold, calculating killer, who knew her legal rights. She may have gone along quietly to the police station but she was not about to confess her evil deeds to Glenn.

Kim Jervis and Tracey Waugh were worried. Neither of them had managed much sleep that night. Their consciences were beginning to get the better of them. And to make matters worse, they had heard about Tracey Wigginton's arrest.

Waugh was the most terrified. At her flat in Clayfield, she cried herself to sleep many hours after the killing of Ted Baldock. She really never wanted any part in the horrific murder.

Jervis — who lived in a separate apartment, also in Clayfield — was equally scared. But she had even more reason. Her knife had been used by Tracey Wigginton in the frenzied attack. She knew it was only a matter of time before the police came looking for her.

Ptaschinski was an all together different animal. She saw the killing and encouraged Wigginton by not trying to stop her murdering Ted Baldock.

To Lisa it had all been a game, a joke. Even now, with the reality of the situation fast encroaching, she still thrilled at the very thought of her love for Bobby.

In Bobby, she had a strong lover with whom she was willing to do anything. As she later told psychiatrist Dr Terry Mulholland: 'If you are going out with someone you do whatever you can to please them.'

The brutal sex. The blood letting. The murder. They were all just part of the thrill of an intense relationship for Lisa. She said later she was infatuated. Obsessive love can cloud judgement. Lisa had lost touch with reality for eight torrid days.

Now she had to try to work out if she knew the real Tracey Wigginton. Not Bobby the he-man, not eight-year-old Tracey and certainly not the Observer. Lisa needed to be able to predict Tracey's behaviour but she never somehow managed that. The fact remained that she couldn't tell if Tracey had started singing to police.

Tracey had had an in-built fear of looking at herself in the mirror since her earliest years. She hated to look at herself. Her confidence had been shattered by the cruel jibes of her step-family. She convinced herself she was ugly and never even bothered to make the effort to smarten herself up.

Her family would frequently punish her for not brushing her hair before school. Tracey began to believe that mirrors were evil objects which reflected her true self — something she could not face up to. Maybe her family were right. Perhaps she was evil. But she didn't really care.

Now here were the police joining a long list of her castigators. She knew just how to act. Calm and detached.

Glenn Burton was puzzled. Having raided Wigginton's flat, it had become blatantly obvious that she was a lesbian living in what locals call 'a dyke's commune'. Even when officers later returned to her flat and found a black cape and other satanic style clothing, they were still baffled.

'After all, black is a trendy colour these days. To link it with vampires seemed somewhat excessive,' explained Glenn later.

Glenn wanted to know why poor old Ted had

stripped down for sex with her by the riverbank. Wigginton was not telling. Her only response was no response. She simply refused to speak.

Glenn feared this was going to be a tough case to crack. He stood over Wigginton as she sat at one of the two desks in the white-walled dayroom at Wooloon Gabba police station.

As the warm midday sunlight dazzled through the office windows, Tracey blinked and squirmed in her seat. It was not the presence of the officers that bothered her, she just felt uncomfortable in direct sunlight. It was a bit like her fear of mirrors and it fuelled the vampire involvement that scandalised Brisbane.

Ironically, on that day, she was relatively well dressed with a pretty white blouse and jeans. Despite the severe haircut she still retained a certain femininity about her.

She'd been there for more than four hours and all they'd got so far was her name and address. But Glenn was still under the impression they needed to find a boyfriend.

The idea of a woman killing at random just did not add up. Men were the cold, calculating murderers. They were the ones who often picked out complete strangers as their victims. No woman could commit such a brutal crime as this. Surely?

Tracey Waugh couldn't take the pressure any more. She had always been the least likely member of the group. Never quite as keen as the others. Always holding back. At one stage her fears led her to believe that Wigginton planned to make her the next blood victim. Waugh was the one who most shied away from the actual murder. She was the one who was close to tears in the back of the car the previous night.

She was painfully aware that Wigginton was sizing her up, imagining the taste of her blood. Or maybe she was lusting after her for sex as well.

Waugh pleaded with Jervis to turn themselves in. As they sat agonising at Jervis' tiny apartment, the two women became increasingly agitated by their situation.

They could not quite believe all this was happening.

Would Wigginton incriminate them?

But at the home of Wendy and Wayne Sugden, Lisa was starting to wonder as well. One moment she imagined that Bobby/Tracey would walk through the door and sweep her off her feet. The next moment she recalled the look of terror on the face of that victim as he was punctured to death.

The Sugdens knew that there was something bothering Lisa. They wanted the truth and they were prepared to coax it out of her. Earlier in the week, she had told them all about Tracey. They were worried. Not only about the lesbian relationship but the fact that Lisa was so easily led. She liked to be dominated and Tracey was definitely doing that.

They were especially concerned when Lisa told

them about the blood lust and Tracey's claims to be a vampire. Now, the look on Lisa's pathetic face said it all. She seemed to be in a trance. Out of touch with everyone and everything.

But that didn't stop the Sugdens being shocked when she blurted out 'Tracey's murdered someone.'

Wendy Sugden was stunned. At first, she failed to comprehend the full meaning of this statement.

'Was it an animal?'

Lisa just muttered: 'A man.'

Wendy and her husband were sickened by what they heard. But they knew instinctively it must be true. They had little difficulty in convincing Lisa to turn herself in to the police that afternoon.

The same dilemma ultimately sealed all their fates. For less than an hour later, Tracey and Kim also walked into the same police station. Until their appearance, Wigginton had sat in stony silence, refusing to co-operate.

If the others had not come forward then maybe Tracey would never have been convicted.

By 1.00am the next morning, an exhausted Glenn Burton left the station for his bayside home having solved what was probably the most horrific killing ever committed by women.

In October 1990, Tracey Wigginton pleaded guilty to the murder of Ted Baldock at Brisbane Supreme Court and was jailed for life.

In February 1991, Lisa Ptaschinski was found guilty of murder and also sentenced to life.

At the same hearing, Kim Jervis was convicted of manslaughter and jailed for eight years.

Tracey Waugh was cleared of murder and freed.

11

The Nymphomaniac Prisoner

She wrapped him in her arms, burying his face in her dark, curly hair. For a moment they rocked back and forth, looking intently into each other's eyes. Then she trailed her tongue from his earlobe to the nape of his neck, stopping every few seconds to kiss and suck his young skin. She licked an imaginary line up a few inches before coming to rest at his ear. There, her tongue probed deeper and deeper. It felt as though she was touching his ear drum, exploring every centimetre before sucking the air from it gently and sensuously.

She was in control. She, the mother of three young children, could do anything she wanted with him. He was six years younger — a virgin until he met her.

Next, she nibbled his earlobe. Five, maybe six, times. He was far too excited to be able to count. They were both standing by the end of the bed, waiting for the right moment to fall backwards onto the soft mattress.

She kissed his chest, circling each nipple with her tongue before biting the end. He winced. The pain was sharp, but pleasant. She looked up at his face to see his reaction. His eyes looked glazed and distant. Her silky lips teased each breast, before sucking in hard.

Domination. That's how she liked it. It gave her more pleasure than anything else.

Her lips started moving further down now, exploring every contour of muscle beneath skin. She ran the tip of her tongue from side to side just above his penis. The lovely, beautiful power of the tease. So near and yet so far.

Finally, after what seemed like years, she went lower. Sucking. Biting. Sucking.

Susan Barber was in ecstasy. She was satisfying her young lover in a way that he could not resist. She could do anything she wanted to him and he would just whimper for more. He was so inexperienced — anxious to learn and receive.

They both fell on to the bed. She paused for a moment, making him lie on his back because she wanted to decide when it was time. Until then, she would tease and caress him to within a flick of a finger before orgasm. Each time his breathing reached fever pitch, she would pull away momentarily, just to make sure he did not come.

Soon she would let Richard get what he so badly wanted. But, until that moment she would continue pushing him to the limit. Watching him squirm with a delight tainted by exasperation.

The unmistakable sound of the front door slamming came from downstairs. Susan stopped dead. It was followed by a crash of cutlery in the kitchen.

'Shit! He's come back early.'

Susan jumped up and grabbed her nylon housecoat from the end of the bed. She could hear her husband coming up the stairs. He had heard something. He was going to find them.

Richard was panic stricken. He was not as fast off the mark as Susan. Also, he had peeled his clothes off in her front room when they had first started kissing.

'Shit!! He's seen the clothes on the floor.'

The bedroom door burst open. Michael Barber was steaming with rage. He had come home early from a fishing trip because of bad weather. It was nothing compared with the storm of fury about to erupt in his house.

There was no point in either of them denying it.

Richard was standing completely naked by the wardrobe, desperately trying to find something to put on. But then he could hardly take out a pair of Michael's trousers!

Susan's nipples pressed hard against the nylon of her housecoat. It was obvious she had nothing else on underneath.

'You whore.'

Michael Barber grabbed at her coat. He wanted to rip it off her, humiliate her. She evaded his grasp and made a dash for the door.

But Michael was not going to let matters rest there.

'Come here, you slut. Come here!'

He yelled abuse at Susan, then he turned his attentions to Richard. Only two days before, the two men had played on the same side in an Essex inter-league darts match at The Plough. Now, that same 'friend' stood before him stark naked after just having made love to his wife in his bed. This was the same man he had bought a pint of bitter for so often. The same man he had congratulated on getting a bullseye. The same man he had encouraged to be patient with the darts team scorer.

'She's not too good at adding up, mate. But her heart's in the right place.'

'She' just happened to be Susan.

'You fucking bastard.'

Michael stood there and looked at Richard's pale and plucked body.

'Pathetic. Fucking pathetic.'

Richard stayed silent — afraid to inflame the situation, not really knowing what to say.

'Now get the fuck out of my house. Bastard.'

Michael tensed his fists in anger. This was an insult to his manhood. His pride. His reputation. He had to do something about it.

'I'm going to kill you.'

He lurched towards Richard, just missing him with his right fist. Still completely naked, the slightly-built lover made a move for the door. He was vulnerable and highly embarrassed, but he had to get out of that house if he valued his own life.

'Come here, you fucking cunt!'

The two men came thumping down the stairs.

Richard slipped, rather than ran, down the stairway, losing his balance every two or three steps in a desperate bid to escape Michael's clutches. In the hallway, he stopped for a moment, but it was a ridiculous idea. There was no way he was going to pick up his clothes from the front room and escape without a beating. They still lay scattered across the carpet where — less than an hour earlier — Susan had so amorously removed them. Richard lunged for the front door.

Michael was gaining on the younger, lighter man. Richard struggled with the front door lock. It was one of those yale-type double locks, almost as difficult to open as to close.

Susan pushed him out of the way and opened the lock for him in one quick motion. She blocked the way while Richard made a run for it. Michael barged his wife out of his path, sending her flying to the floor.

As he reached the front door step, he saw Richard's naked form desperately fiddling with the garden gate. He gave up and hurtled over it in one precarious leap.

Michael knew he would get away. He stopped

chasing and watched as the nude figure ran four houses up Osbourne Road, then went up the pathway to the neighbouring house.

Michael looked at his wife.

'Now it's your turn, bitch …'

He shut the front door and hit his wife across the face.

Michael and Susan were barely on speaking terms the next morning. By the time he left the house to go to work at the nearby Rothman's factory, the atmosphere had got so tense that she had genuinely feared for her life.

The previous night he had beaten her black and blue. She couldn't face another thrashing. Rather than inflame the situation any further, she kept quiet. Praying he wouldn't pick a rematch with her.

Within minutes of watching her husband leave their modest three-bedroomed semi, she found herself thinking about Richard. He kept her going. She wanted to be with him the whole time.

There was not a lot of other happiness in her life at that time. Richard satisfied her craving for physical love. Sex was something that had been missing from her marriage for at least five years. Now she had got her sense of adventure back. She loved to feel that she was doing something exciting. Daring. Naughty.

She always felt so good when she was with him. He made her feel ten years younger than her twenty-nine years — and that was the best part of all. She could relive her lost youth by behaving as irresponsibly as she wanted.

Now, her husband had gone off to work and she wanted her lover once more. She stood by the telephone in the hallway, wondering if she should call him. Would he even want to see her again after what happened yesterday? Perhaps he'd want to finish their affair. After all, he must have been pretty scared. But then again he had left his clothes. That gave her an excuse to call.

She picked up the phone.

Susan and Richard lay next to each other in bed. Both were entirely satisfied. Content for the first time in days. Physically drained from an hour of energy-sapping love making.

'He's mad you know. One day he'll kill you,' said Richard.

Susan knew her lover was right. She had long harboured an intense hatred for her husband. The beatings. The verbal abuse. The lack of affection. The list of reasons why their marriage was in shreds was endless.

She had promised herself she'd leave him. But she'd never plucked up the courage to actually do it. Now, however, it was different. Her infidelities were out in the open and he would become even more violent towards her. He wouldn't be able to understand her need for sex. He'd given it up so why should she have it? That was just the way he saw life. Revolving around him.

Now his pride had taken a battering. The whole

street probably knew what had happened that night. A naked man runs out of their house with the husband in hot pursuit. And he just happens to be the boy who lives with his parents a few doors up the road. The evidence was there for everyone to see.

It would be the talk of the neighbourhood, if not the whole of Westcliff-on-Sea, by now. Susan didn't care. Her need to be loved far outweighed her reputation amongst a load of petty, nosey neighbours. But he would.

As she lay there next to Richard, she began to realise that maybe there was only one solution to the problem. 'Kill him before he kills me.'

She got out of the bed and put on her clothes. Richard looked disappointedly at her. She beckoned him to come with her. They had some very important business to attend to.

The Barber back garden was not exactly an impressive example of horticultural skills. A few flower beds dotted about the place, a scrap of grass in the middle, badly worn by the antics of three young children and a few toys scattered haphazardly beside a climbing frame in the corner.

It was a garden all the same. And nearly all the gardens in Osbourne Road had one thing in common — a shed. They were a vital part of keeping up with the Joneses. The sort of shed you had was a definite reflection of your wealth. Neighbours would frequently glance along the rows of gardens, comparing their own outhouse with those in every garden for at least 100 yards in each direction.

Michael Barber's shed wasn't perfect. But it certainly had a lot of character to it. He had built it with his own fair hands out of slats of wood he got when he worked for a firm of landscape gardeners. About eight feet square, it had another very important role to play besides being the place where he kept all the tools and utensils. It was his very own, very private retreat. A place where he could get away from everything, where neither the children nor the wife could bother him.

He would often spend hours fiddling with bits of car engines in the shed, happy in the knowledge that no one would disturb him. It was the perfect place to escape if you happened to live in a town like Westcliff-on-Sea.

Now, Susan Barber was trying to find out if that shed held the ultimate escape route for her.

With Richard by her side, she was trying to find the Paraquat poison she knew her husband had left in the shed a few years back.

She remembered the day he got it, back in the seventies, because he brought it home from work and used to go on and on about making sure the kids got nowhere near it. They were younger then.

'It's a killer, this stuff. Just remember that.'

Susan had never forgotten her husband's warning.

She took great care as she heaped tablespoonfuls

of the powder into a small pill bottle.

Richard smiled as he watched her.

Susan had taken full heed of her husband's warning by using a bottle with a child-proof cap. You didn't want it getting into the wrong hands, after all.

Susan made an effort for Michael when he came home from work that evening. She wanted to make amends. Start all over. Try and make the next few weeks as bearable as possible. They might be his last.

She made his favourite dish for tea — steak pie. If there was one thing that just about brought a smile to his face, she thought, it was steak pie.

It needed to be cooked for hours beforehand, to make the meat as tender as possible. Michael would never allow her enough money to buy the good meat. She had to make do with that tough stuff that the butchers virtually gave away. But, after simmering for a long time, no one could really tell the difference. At least that's what Michael always said.

Earlier that afternoon, Richard gave her a warm embrace as they stood by the cooker. Together, they were hatching a plan that could give her the perfect way out of an awful marriage.

She picked up the plastic pill container, untwisted the lid and sprinkled the powder into the gravy she was mixing on the stove.

'How much do you think? Is that enough?'

'No. Put some more in. He won't be able to tell the difference.'

Richard hugged his lover, giving her an extra tight squeeze as she dropped most of the contents into the gravy.

He won't humiliate me ever again, she thought.

Michael was not particularly impressed with his favourite dish when he eventually got home from work. He was still seething with anger about the events of the day before. Furious and unforgiving. How could she expect him to just forget the fact that, only twenty-four hours earlier, he had come home and found her in bed with one of the neighbours? What difference could a bloody pie make?

Mind you, he was starving hungry — and that steak pie did smell delicious. Susan always cooked great pies.

It must have covered three quarters of the white plate. The yellowing, crusty pastry contrasting with the dark brown, almost black, colour of the beef. The peas and boiled potatoes were like an afterthought really. Barely making an impression, compared with the vast quantity of pie.

Susan watched him pouring the gravy over the food.

She found she just could not keep her eyes off it. For a moment, Michael looked up at her quizzically.

'What you looking at woman?'

Susan smiled and got back to her own dish of food. She never did like gravy anyway. She always made it especially for her husband.

Michael was a messy eater. He tended to hold his knife and fork like two drum sticks and shovel the food into his mouth. Usually, Susan would grimace with disgust while watching him stuff his face. But this time she actually found herself enjoying the sight of him eating. Munching and then noisily swallowing each gigantic mouthful. It was a lovely sight.

She tried to keep her head down in silence. That was the way it was normally at meal times. Every so often, though, she allowed her eyes to travel discreetly towards his plate of food, where he was feasting on that very special pie.

It didn't take a lot to get Susan excited when she was in a room with an attractive man. Her husband had long since stopped having that effect on her. However, as she sat at the kitchen table, watching Michael devouring his food, she felt a strange tingling sensation rushing through her body. She kept fidgeting in her chair in the hope it would divert his attention from her obviously excited state.

Crossing her legs one moment. Uncrossing them the next. She had to clench her teeth to stop herself from giggling. She could not believe he was actually eating it without a word of complaint.

Richard had said he wouldn't taste a thing. She hadn't believed it. She thought it would surely have had some sort of aftertaste.

But her grotesque lump of a husband was loving each and every mouthful.

'Got any more of this stuff on the go?'

That was the nearest he had come to a compliment in years. She took his plate and piled on yet more pie with a sparse sprinkling of vegetables and sloshed the whole lot with gallons of gluey gravy.

Her breathing had quickened. Would he notice?

No. He was too busy filling his fat stomach.

'What's for sweet then?'

Susan snapped out of her trance. It was probably just as well.

She served up his pudding, happy in the knowledge she had just sentenced her husband to a slow and agonising death.

Susan was irritated.

It had been three days now and there had been no sign of it taking effect. She lay in bed next to her husband wondering if she would have to give him even more Paraquat. Richard had warned it would take a few days.

She could not stand the waiting. Not knowing if his cast-iron stomach had already managed to flush every trace of poison out.

How much longer would it take? She had given him a massive dose. Surely he would start to suffer soon?

Maybe they should have cut his brake cables instead. That would have been much faster and simpler. None of this cooking and waiting around.

As she lay there, she became aware that her husband was stirring. She kept her eyes tightly shut in case he realised she was awake.

It was the middle of the night. He could hardly breath. His throat felt as if it had a layer of carpet clogging it up. His chest was pulsating with pain. What he did not realise was that his lungs had been rapidly turning hard and leathery — making it more and more difficult for any air to get through. Then he started to get awful stabbing pains in his kidneys.

He got up to get a glass of water. But the liquid just made the stinging sensation even more unbearable. He felt as if hundreds of tiny daggers were travelling through his body, stabbing his insides at every opportunity.

Every few moments, his body would twitch with discomfort as the stabs became more and more frequent.

'Susan. Wake up. I'm in fucking agony. Call the doctor.'

Susan Barber thought she was dreaming at first. But no. Her husband's anguished face looked very real.

'At first we thought it was pneumonia, Mrs Barber.' The doctor was full of sympathy for Susan as they stood by the hospital bedside. She had called the ambulance when Michael had collapsed on the bathroom floor.

Slowly. Ever so slowly, she dialled the

emergency services. She didn't want to hurry in case the end was near.

Wouldn't it be great if he died here and now, she thought for a moment. But he was still struggling for life when the ambulance men eventually turned up. Maybe it would be even easier if he died in hospital. Less mess. Less questions. Less suspicion.

In any case, nearby Southend had a perfectly pleasant hospital. Good, clean wards and caring nurses. What more could he ask for? But then Michael Barber was hardly in a fit state to appreciate the nurses!

The poison was now definitely beginning to kill Michael Barber. To him, it must have felt as though a psychopath had been let loose inside his body. Travelling to every corner of his system, ruthlessly mutilating every living organ for no apparent reason.

Now, the doctor in the hospital sounded hesitant about the illness. Perhaps he suspected it was poison. Maybe they were trying to put her to the test. Watching her reaction for any signs of fake concern. Had they found traces of poison in his bloodstream already?

For just a brief moment, Susan was worried. But then she thought, where are the police if they suspect? She glanced around her. No one was approaching with handcuffs. No one was even looking in her direction. She knew she was still in the clear.

The facade of concern for her husband's well-being should not slip for one moment. She had to keep up the pretence. She must not give them any clues.

The doctor at Southend Hospital looked most concerned. Susan wondered what he was about to say.

'We think it may be a condition called Goodpasture's Syndrome. It's a rare nervous disorder that breaks down the body's internal mechanism.'

Susan was confused. Luckily, her confusion helped make her look even more like a heartbroken wife, whose husband was on his death bed.

It was 1981. The AIDS epidemic had not really begun to take its devastating toll on the western world, otherwise the doctors probably would have suspected he was an HIV victim.

Susan was touched by the doctor's concern. It was so nice of him to be so caring. If only he knew she really did not give a jot.

Susan just hoped and prayed he wasn't such a good doctor that he might find out her husband had been poisoned. Worse still, he might even save Michael's life. That really would not do.

'We recommend he is transferred to a special hospital where they can keep an even closer eye on him.'

She did not care where it was, so long as he hurried up and died.

At the beginning of June, Michael Barber was transferred to the Hammersmith Hospital in West London. It had been less than one month since Susan had laced his gravy with Paraquat poison.

On June 27th, he died a dreadful, painful death. The cause was given as pneumonia and kidney failure.

It was only a small service. Susan, the kids and a handful of friends and relatives.

He would have wanted it that way.

Whether he would have welcomed his wife's lover, Richard, with such open arms was perhaps not so certain.

However, Susan needed him there. He was her support — even though they could not stand too close together in case other people noticed.

Instead, they looked at each other longingly as the coffin trundled slowly into the crematorium oven. The organ music played a timeless hymn in the background and the oak casket slid through the curtain. The final memory of her husband: burning in a box of wood.

She had insisted on the crematorium. It meant there would be no body to re-examine. No doubting doctor could exhume his corpse and find fresh clues. He was gone forever. No one would find out.

Now she and Richard could go and get drunk and celebrate. The £16,000 pension and the £900 a year allowance for the kids should take care of them for a while. It had all been so easy.

At Hammersmith Hospital, Professor David Evans had a nagging suspicion about the death of Michael

Barber. He had carried out a detailed post mortem the day after his death. He even took test samples from the body. Blood, urine, everything he could think of, just in case there were signs of Paraquat. He removed vital organs and ordered them to be preserved in jars and kept in storage.

All the signs were there. It had to be. Why else would a perfectly healthy 35-year-old man collapse and die.

Professor Evans reckoned the tests were a mere formality. Once the results arrived back, he would contact the police and tell them to arrest the wife immediately.

He was stunned when they did come back from the National Poisons Unit. There were definitely no signs of Paraquat poisoning. The Professor could not believe it. But he had to take the word of analysts. Even so, he still felt a nagging doubt.

Something about the case did not add up.

There was nothing he could do about it now. Death was through natural causes — the death certificate said so. He would have to drop the case.

'Aren't you bothered what the neighbours think?'

There were times when Richard was shocked by Susan. She just didn't seem to care. She had no pride. He may have been younger than her, but she was the one with the irresponsible streak. The one who was wild and untamed.

It was the day after her husband's funeral, but she couldn't wait a moment longer to have him to herself. She insisted he bring his belongings around and move into the house. He had no choice.

Susan had got away with murder. Now she could enjoy her life for the first time in years. She didn't give a damn what people thought. No one suspected her. It was the perfect crime. Now she wanted her reward — and it came in the shape of Richard. He was the young lover she did all this for. He was the man she wanted in her bed.

Richard, however, was not so keen. It had all started as a casual affair. He'd been swept up by the whole thing.

When they first met at The Plough, he didn't even realise what was on her mind. After all, he was a kid still living at home. She was a happily married mother of three children.

Richard had always lived with his parents. Sheltered from the outside world, he had never even slept with a girl. When his mates in The Plough told him that she had a definite soft spot for him, he thought they were kidding.

When she asked him round one afternoon while Michael was out working a day shift at the nearby Rothmans factory, he went in all innocence — convinced that any fantasies he had about her would not actually come true. She wanted him to fix the fridge. He was more than happy to oblige.

The boys at the pub had already told her he was still a virgin. The idea of seducing an innocent really appealed to her. Richard was even more willing to oblige when she offered to take him to bed.

Six months later, however, he was starting to grow tired of her. She had taught him so much about sex. But now he wanted to try it out with someone new. He didn't want the full time commitment of a live-in relationship — especially with a woman who had just murdered her husband. But Richard was weak and impressionable. That was why she had got him in the first place. He didn't have the courage to tell her what he thought. He just accepted the situation and moved into her house.

It was obvious it would never last.

Professor David Evans was growing more and more fascinated by the Michael Barber case. He kept going back to his findings and re-examining the facts, just in case he had made a mistake. He was looking for something more that would tell him for certain his suspicions were unfounded. He just would not accept the situation. It kept niggling at him. He knew he had to drop the case from his full-time agenda but that did not mean he had to forget it altogether. However hard he tried, he couldn't come up with an explanation of why Barber actually died.

The inquest might have concluded it was natural causes, but Professor Evans knew otherwise. Even if it wasn't poison, it was certainly a fascinating case and he thought it would be intriguing for some of his colleagues to study it.

With the furthering of medical science in mind, he decided to call a conference, the following January, of all the doctors involved in the case — more than six months after the death of Michael Barber.

At least they could swap notes and compare findings. Something that might help save lives in the future.

Susan Barber was bored. She was fed up with being the dominant one in her relationship with Richard. Why couldn't he make a few decisions for a change? Surely he could start acting like a real man rather than a wimp? Maybe it was time to swap him for a more mature model? At least Michael had had a bit of character. Shame, in a way, that he was no longer around.

She laughed at her own ludicrous notions. Michael was the last person she wanted back on this earth.

They were drifting apart. More and more, she was thinking about other attractive men. It was how she felt when she was married to Michael.

It was time to end it — and get out there and start enjoying life once more. Wasn't that exactly what she told herself when Michael was still alive?

Richard was only too happy to go back to his parents, four doors away. They might as well have been a world apart.

Susan needed a new man if she was going to satisfy her never-ending lust for life. Meeting them was not easy in Westcliff-on-Sea. A small, rather drab Victorian seaside resort, it was filled with pensioners living out their last few years. Hardly the sort of place for a merry widow to find an energetic young lover.

Susan was going crazy with frustration. She needed the comfort and support of a man. But, most of all, she needed the physical pleasures. That was what kept her sane. She thought of sex frequently. She needed to satisfy that demand. But how could she do that in a place like Westcliff?

Strangely enough, she eventually found the answer in citizen band radio. Susan had hardly touched the CB set since Michael's death. Now she had an urge to switch it on. She would find herself a man. First, she had to think up a call sign.

'Nympho' seemed appropriate.

Steel erector Martin Harvey always considered himself fit and healthy, but even he was having trouble keeping up with Susan Barber. They had met in the pub only a few hours earlier but it was clear from the start what Susan was after. Everyone knew what Susan liked to do with men.

'She'll eat you for breakfast, mate,' said one helpful soul.

In the pub, she cuddled up to twenty-year-old Martin and told him exactly what she wanted. Richard had gone. She wanted him to share her bed with her, give him her own unique taste in pleasure.

Within seconds of arriving at the house, she had ripped his clothes off and got down to business in front of the electric fire. The first time was pretty traditional but, three hours later, she still had not stopped.

The bathroom. The kitchen. The toilet. The spare bedroom. There was no room left in the house where they had not done it.

Then Susan decided she wanted to try something new.

Leaving Martin lying naked on the bed, she walked over to the corner of the room and switched on the CB transmitter.

'Nympho here ...'

She soon found a willing partner. She told him to turn up the volume and listen. She put the microphone on the table by the bed and got back on top of Martin and started to make love to him.

She whispered in his ear not to make a sound. She wanted her CB pal to think she was having sex with him on the airwaves.

She moaned and sighed. Then she turned her head towards the mike and said: 'Can you hear me ... I'm coming ... harder... harder ... I want you to come too.'

A few days later she was back on the CB again.

'Hello. This is Nympho calling Magic Man. Do you read me ... over?'

Her provocative name would attract the right sort of man.

'Magic Man' turned out to be Rick Search. He had built up quite a rapport with 'Nympho' — now he wanted to meet her in the flesh.

The garage mechanic liked the sound of 'Nympho'. He had that feeling she would live up to her name. He had been surprised, but hardly complained, when she suggested a date. He agreed without hesitation.

Most of the lonely women who broadcast on the CB airwaves tended to be grandmotherly figures just looking for someone to talk to. But 'Nympho' wasn't after a friendly chat. She positively oozed sex down the microphone.

She had decided it was a great way to meet new lovers.

Rick had no doubts what to expect when he called round at her house in Osbourne Road.

He was not disappointed. The magic was definitely there.

Susan was really enjoying the freedom her CB romances allowed her. Most of the men were just interested in one thing — and that suited her. She loved the excitement of meeting men on blind dates. She would wait at the window to her house and watch them arrive. If they were not her type then she would simply pretend to be out.

They'd soon go away. Convinced that 'Nympho' must have been a crackpot who never meant a word of all the sexual innuendo she had spoken over the airwaves.

The merry widow was having the time of her life.

It was now January 1982.

At Hammersmith Hospital, Professor David Evans had assembled the team of doctors who worked on the strange case of Michael Barber. Before them lay a bizarre collection of the dead man's organs and bodily fluids, which had been pickled and stored away.

The doctors began a minute, piece by piece examination of every bit of evidence. They looked at slides that showed Barber's body. They studied the photos of his organs. Then they dissected the actual remains. It was a macabre gathering. But Professor Evans believed it had to be done.

The doctors concluded there were still many unanswered aspects to the case — but there was not enough evidence to re-open it. What baffled them was how Barber could have consumed the Paraquat in the first place. Since 1975, it had been deliberately manufactured with a pungent smell. No one could have taken it without almost immediately vomiting from the awful aroma.

But, as a final gesture, they all agreed that leftover blood and urine samples should be sent to Paraquat manufacturers ICI and the National Poisons Unit.

Some of the medics argued that tests had always proved negative. But Professor Evans just wanted to make doubly sure ...

Two months later, the results came back.

This time they were affirmative. Michael Barber had been poisoned. The original tests had never taken place. All those months earlier, a laboratory technician had wrongly informed Hammersmith Hospital the tests were negative.

In April 1982, Susan Barber and Richard Collins were arrested in Osbourne Road. On November 8, 1982, at Chelmsford Crown Court, Susan Barber was sent to jail for life after being found guilty of murdering her husband.

Former lover Richard Collins was sentenced to two years for conspiring with Susan Barber to kill her husband.

12

Cold Fury

Her hair was thick, lustrous and so dark it might have been spun on the same loom as the night. Her shoulders and back were slender. Her legs were turned to one side, covered up to mid-thigh by sheer black stockings. The curve of her calves was distinct and, under different circumstances, might well have been considered sexually appealing.

The shapely legs, the full hips, the trim waist, the full breasts — all were fully exposed. But it was her face that gave it all away.

The matt grey eyes stared blankly into the moonlight. The rain pelted on to her face then ran down her breasts, exposed by the ripped open blue nurse's uniform that partially covered her lily-white body. Her pubic hair was soaked by the rain, her underwear long since removed. At the back of her head was a small hole rimmed with a black burn mark — the only evidence of assault.

There was no-one else at Broat's Farm. Just a corpse in the muddy yard as the rain slammed hard against the ground on that bitterly cold December evening.

The body of nurse Jayne Smith lay there uncovered. It was an undignified death for anyone. The apparent victim of an horrific sexual assault. Something that no woman could ever wish on her worst enemy.

A tiny beam of light from the farmhouse illuminated the lower half of the corpse, highlighting the tops of her thighs and glistening against her drenched stockings.

The whole scene seemed staged, as if some movie director would emerge from the shadows and shout 'Cut' so the actress could get up and walk back to her trailer for a fresh application of make-up. But the body did not stir. And the film crew never materialised.

A car came around the corner into the entrance to the farm. As the headlights panned across the yard, they momentarily picked out the body. The car jerked to a sudden halt. The driver scrambled out, leaving the door swinging on its hinges, and slid through the muddy yard to the crumpled body of Jayne Smith.

Before he even reached her body, William

Smith knew she was dead. There was no movement. The body was twisted slightly out of shape. His wife of just seven months lay, lifeless, in front of him. For a few moments, he just blinked. Unable to absorb the awfulness of what had happened. He squeezed his eyes tightly shut in the hope that when he opened them again, she would be gone — back inside their farmhouse, making him supper lovingly. Smiling at him lovingly. Being a good wife lovingly.

She was still there. Abused and dead.

William knelt in the puddle beside her body, immune to the icy wind that swept up from the North Yorkshire moors. He took her hand in his. Desperate for one last response before she was taken from him for ever.

He felt her fingers. The nails. The softness of the skin that had been so very much alive just a few hours before.

He squeezed her hand tightly. The cold clamminess did not matter. At least he was here, with her, showing how much he really loved and cared for her.

He moved his hand further down into her palm, pressing tight. Something was missing. But in the emotional turmoil that had occurred during the past few minutes, he could not make out what it was.

He moved his hand up towards her fingers once more. Despite the tears that welled up in his eyes and throbbing pain of tension in his head, he kept feeling her hand. Why this? He had to know. He had to know.

He looked down at the limp discoloured fingers. And he realized with a jolt what was missing.

Her wedding ring.

Somehow his numb fingers punched in the three numbers.

'You've got to help me.'

After a few seconds, a WPC came on the line. She sensed it immediately. She could tell that this was genuine.

'My wife has been murdered at home. I have just got in.'

His voice was straining all the time. It was almost impossible to say that word. Murdered. It thumped the truth home to him.

He wasn't sure if he could continue with the call. What was the point? Nothing was going to bring Jayne back. No amount of sympathy. No miracle cure. She had gone forever.

William was a pragmatic man. As a child, he had always been taught to bottle up his emotions and never cry in public. 'Men don't do that sort of thing, son,' his father once told him. But now he wanted to shed floods of tears. Let his emotions loose on the phone to a complete stranger. What would his folks have said to that?

He had to continue. He took a deep breath.

'She's laid in the yard. There is blood all over.'

Blood. Just one word. It was there. It was real. His voice was really choking now. He just didn't know if he could go through with it.

She was dead. There was no future without her. How could he carry on?

Another deep breath gave him just enough courage. 'Her clothes have been removed and she looks as though she has been raped and murdered.'

He slammed the phone down after spitting out the words. It was the first contact he had had with anyone since the discovery. Now he knew it really was actually happening. The nightmare had begun.

Yet just seven months earlier, this dreadful episode wouldn't have seemed possible to twenty-eight-year-old Jayne Wilford and farmer William Smith, seven years her senior.

Their wedding had been beautiful. Held at a church in the heart of the North Yorkshire Moors, it had seemed like a scene out of Wuthering Heights. Farmers and their families gathered for a really happy occasion in a picturesque setting.

Although it was May 1988, it could easily have been any time this century. Time does not seem to catch up with anything in that part of the world. Relatives and friends were convinced the happy couple would be together until they died. They had that feeling about them.

They seemed to go so well together.

William, a shy, bearded, hard working man of the land. Jayne, the caring, outgoing nurse who looked forward to having a family by the man she first fell for when she was still at school.

They say opposites attract each other to make the perfect marriages. In their case, it looked like it was true.

Yet it could all have been so very different for William.

Just over a year earlier, he had been due to marry another, older woman when Jayne stepped back into his life.

Yvonne Sleightholme had wanted William from the first moment she clapped eyes on him, at a rugby club disco on New Year's Eve, 1979. Beneath her rather staid clothes and practical hairstyle, lurked a ruthlessly determined woman.

William had always been a bit of a slow starter, so she had to make the running in every sense of the word.

At first, William was happy to be led by Yvonne. She was a brittle, strong Yorkshire lass. Always planning every moment they had together. Nothing was too much for Yvonne. She enjoyed running his life for him.

It meant she could take control. She decided who they did and did not see. Which of his friends were in and which were out.

Yvonne had big plans for them, including marriage.

William didn't even think about it at first. His world stopped at the gates to Broat's Farm. He just let her carry on with the arrangements. He kept meaning to take a step back and consider it all, but it was a busy time on the farm and he never got the chance. He just wanted a peaceful life. Married or not. It didn't make a whole lot of difference to him.

After eighteen months of courtship, he did not mind the idea of a wedding. He was approaching his thirties. Most people in those parts took the plunge by then.

Gradually, however, it dawned on him that marriage to Yvonne might not be such a good idea. She was brilliant at running his life. But surely there had to be more to love than just that? True, she had moved into his farm and it was nice to have a woman around. But marriage?

He took her out one day and quietly, but tactfully, told her it was over between them.

She was stunned. She had been about to book the wedding arrangements. How could he turn around and dump her without any warning? There wasn't even anyone else.

Regular churchgoer Yvonne saw in William someone she genuinely felt she could love and cherish for the rest of her life. Someone who was soft, gentle and considerate. Someone completely malleable. She was not going to let him go that easily.

A few weeks later, she insisted they meet for one last time.

William agreed because he did not want to hurt her feelings. He soon began to wish he hadn't.

'I've got leukaemia — and it's all your fault.' Yvonne was shouting, close to tears, at William. 'It's got worse since you finished with me. You've got to do something.'

William was speechless. Here was the woman he had cleanly and kindly tried to finish a relationship with, insisting that he had sentenced her to death by not continuing their affair.

He didn't expect a lot out of life. But why was she saying these things? It wasn't his fault, surely? But William was a trusting sort of bloke and Yvonne Sleightholme convinced him it was all his fault. Riddled with guilt, he agreed to carry on their courtship. He could not bear to see anyone so ill. Perhaps there was a chance she might recover now, he thought.

Miraculously, all traces of the illness disappeared within weeks of them getting back together. And William even began to think that maybe they did belong to each other. Perhaps fate had meant them to get together again? She was a good woman after all.

So William was hardly surprised when Yvonne began making new arrangements for a wedding.

This time, she told herself, he won't get away.

'I want this wedding,' she said. 'It is going to happen. It is going to be the most beautiful day of my life.'

Yvonne was in her element. Being a doctor's receptionist was clearly taking second place to her latest career — organising her forthcoming marriage.

The date was set six months ahead to give her ample time to sort out the church, the dress, the reception, the honeymoon. It was all very time-consuming and Yvonne did so love to organise …

Meanwhile, William carried on working hard at the farm, rarely having time to go out except to attend the countless fittings for his morning suit and to see the vicar to discuss the ceremony.

On one rare, fateful trip into the nearby town of Salton, he bumped into his old friend Jayne Wilford.

They had once been very close. But both had drifted off into different directions after she had reached her twenties. William often thought about what had happened to Jayne. But she always seemed to have a new boyfriend on her arm whenever he saw her. She seemed to have outgrown him or so he presumed.

Jayne had heard about the wedding plans and wanted to give him her congratulations. There was, of course, another motive for seeking him out. She also thought a lot about William.

'You know. I always reckoned that one day we would get married. It has always been one of my secret dreams.'

William was shocked but at the same time, pleased. It was exactly what he hoped she would say. There had always been something special between them. They might have drifted apart years before, but there was always a feeling that destiny might play a hand in bringing them together once more.

Jayne wasn't just trying to steal another woman's husband-to-be. She had a chilling message to deliver to the man she really loved more than anyone else.

'I think you are being conned into a relationship that you know is not right for you.'

William listened intently. In the back of his mind these were the very things he feared about his impending marriage to Yvonne.

Jayne went on, 'You are being dragged into a relationship by someone who is lying and scheming.'

William nodded his head in agreement. He knew that every word she was saying was true. Yet how could he break off his relationship with Yvonne? He was well aware of the hurt he would cause.

For a few weeks, William was in a complete quandary. Every time he started to tell Yvonne that it was off, she would override the conversation with her prattle about the arrangements for the wedding.

William then did something he had never contemplated ever doing in his life. He began sleeping with Jayne while still involved with Yvonne. He was unable to break the news to Yvonne. It was a remarkable sham. And he hated himself for it. It tormented him.

Betrayal did not come easily to William. Some men cheat all their lives, but William had never done it. Now the strain of keeping up a relationship with two women at the same time was tearing him apart emotionally. He could not stand it. He knew it was wrong. And it was impossible to know if

Yvonne realised. She just seemed so wrapped up in those damned wedding arangements.

Yvonne's family were delighted their daughter had at last found happiness. She had lived at home on their farm for so long they had been worried she might remain a spinster for life. William seemed such a lovely character.

It was all yet more pressure on him. Making it more and more difficult to come clean. Yvonne had long since moved into his farm, making herself busy putting her own inimitable female stamp on the decor. Choosing new curtains, kitchen equipment and other essentials that had always been missing when William lived there alone.

He was guilty of cowardice and he knew it. By letting her continue to think he was willing to marry, he was just getting deeper and deeper into trouble.

Jayne kept urging him. Aware of what it must be like for the other woman. She was just as uncomfortable with this blatant deception. She kept thinking how she would have felt if the situations were reversed.

Then it happened. The one thing no one ever plans for, but everyone dreads just before a wedding. Yvonne became pregnant. She became distraught because she might not fit into the wedding dress. For days she told no one her secret. Fearful of the shame it might bring on them, but especially worried about that dress. In North Yorkshire, they still frowned upon children conceived outside marriage.

All the tension had tragic consequences

because, within a few days, she had miscarried. No one knew about the baby except her doctor.

Meanwhile, William was wracked with guilt about his affair with Jayne. He decided he had to tell her the truth.

'I've found someone else. I just don't think it would be right to carry on. Let's finish it for good this time.'

He was trying to be honourable. He had confessed his deception and now he just wanted them to finish peacefully. He knew he had done wrong. But he was coming clean. Telling the truth was the only way he knew. He felt it had gone on for quite long enough.

Yvonne was devastated. The hurt was immeasurable. She was still in love with him. She was just weeks from marrying him. What could she tell their relatives and friends?

But, perhaps worst of all, she had just lost his baby — and he hadn't even known she was pregnant. She needed his love and support through her difficult time. She didn't want to hear that the man she was about to marry had fallen in love with another woman.

'I have just miscarried our baby.'

William didn't know what to do. This was turning into an even more difficult situation. After her last attempt to keep him through lies, he didn't even know if she was telling the truth.

He felt awful, but no amount of sympathy would bring them back together yet again. He still couldn't marry her.

'I no longer have any desire for you. Don't you understand?'

It was hurting William almost as much as it was hurting her. But it had to be said.

'We have both tried so hard but it hasn't worked out. I want to be free to find out how I truly feel about Jayne.'

William's words were so carefully put — even at such a crucial moment. Yvonne knew she could do nothing but accept that it was over, though underneath the polite, civilised conversation, she was nurturing a resentment and hatred that would bring horrific consequences.

Just a few months later Jayne Milford moved into Broat's Farm.

The ghost of Yvonne Sleightholme had not yet been finally laid to rest. Unable to accept that it was completely over, she hadn't removed any of her belongings at first. It was as if she was convinced that William and Jayne would part and she could just carry on where she left off.

When she did eventually turn up, three months later, to gather her things, the atmosphere was strained and difficult. The three of them hardly uttered a word.

She soon left. Drove away from the farm, out of their lives forever. They hoped.

The voice at the other end of the phone line was menacing and cold.

'I'm going to kill you, bitch …'

There was a click and the line went dead.

Jayne Smith had just returned with new husband William after their honeymoon.

Everyone gets cranky calls sometimes. But the voice seemed familiar.

No. It couldn't be her, thought Jayne. It was all over long ago. No one could harbour such intense resentment, surely? When she told William, he dismissed it in much the same way. The Smiths were a happy, trusting couple. They didn't really see the bad side of anyone. They didn't want to.

'Quick. Quick. There's a fire in the barn.'

William rushed out into the yard. For almost half-an-hour he bravely dampened down the blaze with water and blankets.

It could have turned into a major catastrophe.

Strange really. He could not work out how on earth it had happened. Then he started to think that maybe it had been started deliberately. Perhaps she was responsible. Then again, no one would go to those lengths. Would they?

'This is it. I've bloody well had enough of this nonsense. I'm going to see the police.'

It was not often that William Smith lost his temper. But this time she had gone too far.

In his hand he held a wreath with a chilling message, 'Jayne. I'll always remember you.'

William was outraged.

'She's sick in the head. She's got to be stopped.'

Domestic disputes don't come high on the police's list of priorities. Nevertheless, under pressure, they agreed to visit Yvonne to see if she was behind the incidents. But they were not that interested. As far as they were concerned, there were real villains to be caught — not lovelorn spinsters.

And when they interviewed Yvonne she really switched on the charm. The two officers came away from her family's farm convinced she was far from a danger to the Smiths. In fact, she seemed like a very nice responsible sort of person. Hardly the type to carry out a vicious hate campaign. And, even if she was behind some of the incidents, a jilted woman making a pest of herself was hardly an unusual occurance. Let the dust settle and she'll soon give up, the police assured William and Jayne.

Shortly after the wreath incident, Yvonne decided enough was in fact enough — she had to clear her head and try to start afresh.

The first stage in this self-induced rehabilitation was to travel across the nearby border into Scotland, hire a holiday cottage and forget about all her problems. She even got herself a new boyfriend.

In ambulance driver Anthony Berry, she had at last found a new man who she felt fond of. At least he satisfied her physically, if not entirely socially. Hidden away in the border country, they could make love until the cows came home. She could put

William and all her troubles behind her.

It would be a wonderful break for them both, she told friends. But, inside, the resentment and hatred still bubbled. She was obsessed with the man who had spurned her. Every time she looked at her lover next to her, she saw William. Every time she walked hand in hand with him through the fields, she saw William.

It was no use pretending. She would have to get him back. Punish that witch Jayne for humiliating her. For making her the laughing stock of all her sneering relatives. For making William turn his back on her when she needed him most.

But by December 14, Yvonne was like a different person. They had been on holiday for over a week and it was as if all the cares of the world had been lifted from her shoulders. She was beaming with delight. Looking radiant. And best of all she was feeling really passionate.

She had been out for a very long drive alone and now she was back at the cottage, demanding sex from Anthony. Anywhere. She just had to have it — then and there.

He began by probing her mouth deeply with his tongue. Then she allowed him to stroke her body gently. She shut her eyes and savoured the waves of pleasure that coursed through her agile body.

She wanted to imagine it was William, not Anthony, exploring her body. She could see his face, above her, satisfying her, kissing her, loving her. It made the actual sex more enjoyable.

As Yvonne lay there enjoying endless pleasures, she cast her mind back to less than 24 hours earlier. It was a vivid recollection and it made her feel even more aroused.

She had laid patiently in wait for William to leave the farm for his regular game of five-a-side football. After all those years together, how could she forget his soccer. Every Tuesday, without fail, he would go off, leaving his ever-so-sweet little wife all alone at the farm to fend for herself. Alone and vulnerable.

From her vantage point just off the road by the corner, Yvonne knew he would have to pass. She watched silently as his car drove down towards the village. Even though she was not close enough to actually see his face through the car window, she felt a sense of excitement just to know she had been near to him once more.

Soon, she would have him back. He would be hers once more.

She waited patiently in her car. Just in case he returned. He might have forgotten a boot or a sock. She could not be too careful. After ten minutes, she knew he had gone for hours.

She got out of the car and took a deep breath. The wind from the moors whistled furiously around her. The rain was stinging her face as it lashed across the road in front of her. Sometimes the ice cold water would sweep up into a virtual whirlwind before landing with a smack on the tarmac of the road.

It was pitch black except for the two room lights that shone out from the farm house. The luminous eyes of a fox glanced right in front of Yvonne. The creature scuttled back into the thick undergrowth by the side of the lane. She paused for a moment, then smiled a knowing sort of smile. A look that said nothing would scare her that night. She glanced up at the farmhouse as a silhouette crossed a window. Sweet little Jayne was in.

As Yvonne walked through the muddy yard towards the front door, she felt a surge of tension go through her body. She was hyped up. Stiff with expectation. She felt that resentment and hatred return once more. It was driving her on all the time, telling her to continue …

She was breathing quite heavily now. In through her nose, out through her mouth. All the time exercising the muscles of her fingers, twirling them as if she were about to play the piano, making sure they were loosened and responsive.

Just two steps from the door, she pushed her hand under her anorak and felt the warm glossy veneer of the wooden handle of the rifle. She pulled it out. It was quite heavy and it took both hands to ease out.

Now she had it pointing downwards with her right hand on the trigger. Her other hand covered the upper end of the barrel. She pressed the doorbell with the end of the rifle. It was a cold, calculating movement.

Yvonne narrowed her eyes and squinted at the

door as she waited for it to open. The gun was now trained dead centre on the entrance.

Jayne was not the sort of person to worry about strangers calling at the house at night time. She had typical country trust — the belief in people's better natures. She could not imagine anyone wishing her harm — even after all that fuss with Yvonne.

Jayne had only just got home from her night shift at the old people's home where she worked as a nurse. There had not even been time to change out of her uniform.

As she pulled open the door, her pretty face filled with surprise at first, rather than fear. It was a symptom of that momentary feeling of disbelief that always occurs when something completely out of the ordinary happens.

She looked straight at Yvonne. Then at the gun. Then stood there, unable to react.

But Yvonne soon broke the silence.

She marched Jayne over to the farmyard. Prodding her constantly with the gun to keep her moving in the direction she wanted. Jayne knew precisely what all this was about.

Yvonne's bitterness had known no limits. Jayne had over-estimated the woman's better nature.

They stood there, buffetted by the torrential rain. No conversation between them. Just a rifle barrel for communication purposes. Pointing right into the back of Jayne's head. It was the waiting that was the worst. Waiting for Yvonne to take control and pull the trigger.

She hesitated — not because she was scared. She just enjoyed the suffering. She wanted to see the pain she was causing. She felt the urge to flex her fingers once more. She held the weapon tight in her grasp, remembering everything she had learnt on the rifle range years before. She didn't want to mess it up. Clean and quick. And oh so beautiful.

Yvonne felt the central muscle on her finger squeezing tightly on the trigger. She felt the barrel quiver as the bullet raced into Jayne's head. In a split second it was over.

Yvonne did not panic. She looked at the crumpled body in the muddy yard and realised there was ample time to avoid being accused of this murder. But first, she had to guarantee that he alone would know that she had done it.

She pulled Jayne's limp left hand off the ground and tried to pull off her wedding band. It would not budge. The torrential rain had swollen her finger. Yvonne could do nothing. For a moment, she panicked. The murder had been too easy. But trying to remove her wedding ring was part of her obsession. She had to get it off — no matter what.

She had to know that Jayne would go to her grave without that ring.

She was Mrs William Smith, not Jayne. That scheming bitch had no rights to him in the first place. She had stolen him from her. Now she was denying her the right to remove that ring.

Yvonne would not give up. She struggled to get the ring off. Finally, she managed to twist and turn it enough to pull it up and off her finger.

Elated at her achievement, she now began to consider her next move. People would think it was her. She had to do something to divert attention away from the obvious. That meant making sure it looked like the work of a man.

She crouched down over the body and ripped open the buttoned front of Jayne's nursing tunic. At first, the well-sewn buttons would not give. But, with one almighty yank, they began to pop apart. She stood up and studied her work. It did not look at all convincing. It had to look like the real thing. Not some feeble attempt at pretending it was rape.

Once again, she bent down. All the time the rain was sweeping across her, sometimes hitting her straight in the face. But she knew there was still more work to be done.

She pulled the dress down off her shoulders and arms. Not stopping for a moment to consider the beauty of the person whose life she had just destroyed. She undid the bra and, flexing those fingers like a concert pianist once more, she squeezed the breasts as hard as possible to leave the sort of marks that would be a clear indication of a sexual motive. Men must do that when they rape women, she presumed.

Yvonne was in her element. She loved the organisation side of it. Getting the scene right meant methodical thought, and she had ample supplies of that.

Next, she removed Jayne's pants, nearly slipping in the thick mud as she did so. She pulled them over Jayne's thighs and down the calves towards her slender ankles revealing drenched black stockings.

It was almost over. But not quite. This was supposed to be a sex attack and one vital detail was missing.

She stuffed the sodden pants into her pocket and then lent down, flexing those fingers for the last time …

Yvonne was close to climaxing as Anthony continued heaving himself up and down on top of her.

Her mind had wandered back from the exquisite events of just 20 hours earlier. It seemed like a fantasy. The only reality was that William would soon be hers once more.

After a sensible period of time, she could see the man she really loved again. Then they could marry. Meanwhile Anthony would do. He was a good lover. Anxious to please. Keen to listen.

She felt as though she were in some warm cocoon. Safe in the knowledge that she had committed the killing and she had done everything to put the police off her scent.

The two police officers were charming. They just

wanted to have a few brief words with Yvonne. Anthony let them in immediately.

He was completely unaware of what his lover had done. Yvonne seemed shocked by the news.

'It can't be true. How awful.'

Yvonne burst into tears when the officers told her. She was clearly distressed and upset. They had been warned to expect her to be hard-nosed and unfeeling about Jayne. But here she was crying profusely. It hardly seemed the reaction of a suspected murderess.

The officers said she certainly did not seem to behave like a suspect.

And William's mother could not believe that Yvonne would do such a thing. After all, she received a delightful Christmas card from her the day after Jayne's death.

Inside was a handwritten note. It said: 'I have a lovely boyfriend. 'He has been with me for quite some time now ... through all the worrying times.'

It seemed to convince everyone that she had put all thoughts of ever marrying William firmly out of her mind.

Yvonne posted it just a few hours before she went to Broat's Farm.

She had been very, very meticulous.

William Smith was distraught.

His life was in ruins. He did not know if Yvonne had murdered his wife or not. He was too numb to care about anything except Jayne.

As he hurried along the busy High Street, he knew he had to do one last thing before they buried his darling, beautiful wife.

He frantically looked up and down the road. It was difficult to concentrate in such a bereaved state. But after a few minutes, he was certain he had found the right shop.

He walked in hesitantly — just in case he was wrong.

But the jeweller recognised him instantly.

'You sold me a ring …'

William started to explain but the man remembered him immediately.

Detective Superintendent Geoff Cash had at last got a breakthrough in the case. Everyone said it must be Yvonne Sleightholme, but the attack seemed to have been carried out by a man with a sexual motive. Then, his officers discovered that she had not been at that cottage in the Scottish borders on the night of the killing.

Then they had found blood stains, matching the victim's group, in Yvonne's car.

Inside the funeral parlour, William Smith walked towards the open coffin — to see his wife for the last time.

She now looked — in death — almost as near to perfection as she had whilst alive.

In a few minutes, they would be taking her

away to the funeral ceremony. But for those last few precious moments, he looked at her, remembering all the good times. The wedding. The happy home they shared together. The smiles. The plans.

William leant over the coffin and gently placed the gold ring on Jayne's finger. Now they had become one again. Not even she could take that from them …

On May 10 1991, Yvonne Sleightholme was jailed for life at Leeds Crown Court.

Shortly after her arrest for the murder of Jayne Smith, she was diagnosed as having gone blind following the trauma of the incident.

Judge Mr Justice Waite told Sleightholme: 'When your fiancé broke off the engagement and married another woman you wrought a terrible revenge upon the newly married couple.'

'You planned in cold fury and executed the killing of your rival with ruthless precision.'

YOU COULD WIN THE AMAZING SLEUTH'S SILVER DAGGER!

The first twelve titles in Blake's True Crime Library series each contain a question relating to the book. Collect the numbered editions of Blake's True Crime Library, and when you have the answers to all the questions, fill in the form which you will find at the back of the twelfth book and send it to Blake Publishing to be entered into the prize draw.

HERE IS THE FIRST QUESTION

What make of car did Norman Modin meet his death?

The winner will receive the exclusive sleuth's silver dagger and five runners-up will receive three free copies of Blake's True Crime Library titles.

How to enter

Fill in the answer form contained in the twelfth book in the series and post it to us. If you have won, we will notify you. Whether you are a winner or not, you will still be eligible for a FREE True Crime Newsletter!

Competition rules

1. The 'How to Enter' instructions form part of the rules.
2. These competitions are not open to any members of Blake Publishing or their families, or Blake Publishing's advertising agents, printers or distributors.
3. The prizes will be awarded, in order of their value, to the senders of the first winning entries after the closing date.
4. Entries must be on the entry coupon supplied and will be not be accepted after the closing date.
5. No claim is necessary, winners will be notified.
6. In cases where a manufacturer discontinues a product which has been specified as a prize, Blake Publishing Ltd will substitute the nearest equivalent model of similar or higher value.
7. The Editor's decision is final, and no correspondence can be entered into.